Internal Relationship Management: Linking Human Resources to Marketing Performance

Internal Relationship Management: Linking Human Resources to Marketing Performance has been co-published simultaneously as *Journal of Relationship Marketing,* Volume 3, Numbers 2/3 2004.

Internal Relationship Management: Linking Human Resources to Marketing Performance

Michael D. Hartline, PhD
David Bejou, PhD
Editors

Internal Relationship Management: Linking Human Resources to Marketing Performance has been co-published simultaneously as *Journal of Relationship Marketing*, Volume 3, Numbers 2/3 2004.

Routledge
Taylor & Francis Group

NEW YORK AND LONDON

First published 2004 by
The Haworth Press, Inc., 10 Alice Street, Binghamton, NY 13904-1580 USA

Published 2015 by Routledge
711 Third Avenue, New York, NY 10017, USA
2 Park Square, Milton Park, Abingdon, Oxon OX14 4RN

Routledge is an imprint of the Taylor & Francis Group, an informa business

Internal Relationship Management: Linking Human Resources to Marketing Performance has been co-published simultaneously as *Journal of Relationship Marketing*, Volume 3, Numbers 2/3 2004.

Cover design by Lora Wiggins

Library of Congress Cataloging-in-Publication Data

Internal relationship management : linking human resources to marketing performance / Michael D. Hartline, David Bejou, editors.
    p. cm.
    "Co-published simultaneously as Journal of relationship marketing, volume 3, numbers 2/3 2004."
    Includes bibliographical references and index.
    ISBN 0-7890-2460-8 (hard cover : alk. paper) – ISBN 0-7890-2461-6 (soft cover : alk. paper)
    1. Marketing–Management. 2. Marketing–Personnel management. 3. Organizational commitment. 4. Job satisfaction. 5. Employee motivation. I. Hartline, Michael D. II. Bejou, David.

HF5415.13.I579 2004
658.8–dc22

2004015938

ISBN 13 : 978-0-7890-2460-2 (pbk)

Internal Relationship Management: Linking Human Resources to Marketing Performance

CONTENTS

ABOUT THE EDITORS

Michael D. Hartline, PhD, is Associate Professor of Marketing in the College of Business at Florida State University. His research focuses on services marketing with a particular emphasis on managing the interfaces between managers and customer-contact employees, and customer-contact employees and customers. Dr. Hartline's research has examined issues such as employee socialization, the dissemination of customer-oriented strategy, and the managerial control mechanisms used to influence the attitudes and job responses of customer-contact employees. His research has appeared in the *Journal of Marketing*, *Journal of Business Research*, *Journal of Relationship Marketing*, and the *Journal of Services Marketing*, among others. He is also a coauthor of a textbook on marketing strategy.

David Bejou, PhD, is Professor of Marketing and Dean of School of Business at Virginia State University. He previously served on the faculty of the University of North Carolina at Wilmington, where he was nominated in 1996 for the Chancellor Teaching Excellence Award, and nominated in both 1995 and 1996 for the Faculty Scholarship Award. He has also been a faculty member at several other universities in the United States and Australia.

Dr. Bejou has published widely in professional journals, including the *Journal of Services Marketing*, the *Journal of Business Research*, the *Journal of Marketing Management*, the *International Journal of Bank Marketing*, and the *European Journal of Marketing*. He is a member of the American Marketing Association and the Academy of Marketing Science, and has been a presenter or Session Chair at many national and international conferences.

Dr. Bejou has served as a marketing/promotions consultant to the United Carolina Bank (UCB), Brunswick Community College, and other businesses and community organizations.

Internal Relationship Management: Linking Human Resources to Marketing Performance

Michael D. Hartline

Florida State University

David Bejou

Virginia State University

This paper focuses on the theme of internal relationship management and the linkages between human resource management and marketing performance. Interdisciplinary research in marketing has been gaining some momentum in recent years as many scholars have noted the intriguing and vitally important linkages between managerial practice and marketing performance. Still, this area of research remains understudied and underdeveloped in the marketing literature. This fact served as the motivation in doing this special volume.

Given the realities of today's competitive business environment, firms are forced to leverage all assets at their disposal in their attempt to differentiate product offerings, offer exceptional quality and value, and deliver on their promises of customer satisfaction. Today, more than ever, firms realize that their most important asset is their people, especially the employees that are responsible for delivering quality, value,

[Haworth co-indexing entry note]: "Internal Relationship Management: Linking Human Resources to Marketing Performance." Hartline, Michael D., and David Bejou. Co-published simultaneously in *Journal of Relationship Marketing* (Best Business Books, an imprint of The Haworth Press, Inc.) Vol. 3, No. 2/3, 2004, pp. 1-4; and: *Internal Relationship Management: Linking Human Resources to Marketing Performance* (ed: Michael D. Hartline, and David Bejou) Best Business Books, an imprint of The Haworth Press, Inc., 2004, pp. 1-4. Single or multiple copies of this article are available for a fee from The Haworth Document Delivery Service [1-800-HAWORTH, 9:00 a.m. - 5:00 p.m. (EST). E-mail address: docdelivery@haworthpress.com].

and satisfaction to the firm's customers. These firms have found that "taking care of customers" requires a focused effort aimed at "taking care of their employees." These efforts include internal relationship management, internal marketing, and finding ways to leverage human resource management activities in an attempt to enhance marketing performance, especially at the frontline of the firm.

The aim of this special volume is to examine internal relationship management, its impact on the attitudes and behaviors of marketing personnel, and its effect on marketing performance. While much of the early and current research in this area takes place in the context of personal selling and services marketing, the questions arising from this research are equally germane in retail, healthcare, manufacturing/ production operations, hospitality, public service, academic, and government settings. Within the scope of the special volume, a number of topics were suggested as potential avenues for research:

- internal relationship development, maintenance, and dissolution
- internal marketing strategies that foster marketing performance
- the role of marketing control mechanisms in managing internal relationships
- the effect of management/leadership strategies on the performance of marketing personnel
- internal communication processes that enhance internal relationship development
- the recruitment, selection, and retention of marketing personnel
- the role of employee socialization and training programs in enhancing marketing performance
- relationships within groups/teams and their impact on marketing performance
- employee evaluation and compensation strategies

Many of these topics have been addressed in the special volume by established and emerging scholars in both marketing and management. The goal of the special issue is to provide an integrated, state-of-the-art perspective on internal relationship management and its effects on marketing performance. Each of the five articles accepted for inclusion in the special volume takes a different path toward achieving this goal.

In the first article, Wood, Glew, and Street present the results of a study that examines boundary spanners' appraisals of career entry transitions. Using a sample of boundary spanners from telecommunications, insurance, manufacturing, accounting, and retail firms, their results indicate that boundary spanners' appraisals are affected by the centrality of their work role, the presence of personal resources to ease the transition, and a sense of coherence that buffers the stressful nature of the transition. These results shed light on ways in which firms can manage the career entry transition–one of the earliest connections in the process of managing internal relationships.

Along the same theme, the second article by Hartline and De Witt examines the recruitment, selection, and retention of customer-contact service employees. In a nationwide survey, the authors examine individual characteristics of contact employees (experience, job tenure, age, and education) and their relationships with important attitudinal and job-response variables. Their results indicate that the most satisfied, committed, and least stressed employees tend to be older, better educated, and possess a great deal of experience. Unfortunately, these employee characteristics are atypical in many service settings, suggesting that managers face a difficult task in recruiting, selecting, and retaining employees that are best suited for customer-contact positions.

In the third article, Stan, Landry, and Evans present a study that examines how internal communication processes affect boundary spanners' satisfaction with organizational support services. These services, such as information systems, market research, training, accounting, and facilities support, are critical in developing and maintaining strong internal relationships that support the efforts of boundary spanners in cultivating external relationships. The results of their study of salespeople indicate that informational consistency, communication frequency, and communication bidirectionality affect boundary spanners' perceptions of support services quality and their satisfaction with support services outcomes. However, boundary spanners' satisfaction with support services outcomes has a more enduring impact on their job satisfaction.

In the fourth article, Miles and Mangold propose a conceptual model of employee branding–an organizational process whereby employees internalize the firm's desired brand image and become motivated to project that image to customers and other external stakeholders. Their arguments center around the importance of the psychological contract between the firm and its employees, the message sources that are carefully managed to build and maintain that contract, and the consequences that result from the process.

In a similar vein, the final article by Lassk, Kennedy, and Goolsby explores the concept of internal customer mind-set, or the importance employees place on serving internal customers. Their study of marketing personnel examines internal customer mind-set as a mediator in the relationship between job satisfaction/organizational commitment and the outcomes of job performance and turnover intentions. The results of their study indicate that job satisfaction and commitment strengthen the internal customer mind-set of marketing personnel. In turn, employees exhibiting a stronger internal focus perform better than employees having a weak internal focus. Turnover intentions are driven more by job satisfaction and commitment rather than an internal customer mind-set.

Together, these articles explore many facets of internal relationship management, particularly in the initial and maintenance stages of firm/employee relationships. While much work remains to be done, our hope is that this collection will set an agenda for future work and prompt others to engage in this important and fascinating area of research. We hope you enjoy the publication as much as we have enjoyed working with this talented group of authors.

The Genesis of Relationships:
Boundary Spanners' Appraisals
of the Career Entry Transition

Charles M. Wood

University of Tulsa

David J. Glew

University of North Carolina at Wilmington

Marc D. Street

University of South Florida at St. Petersburg

Charles M. Wood, PhD, is Assistant Professor of Marketing, University of Tulsa, 600 South College Avenue, Tulsa, OK 74104 (E-mail: charles-wood@utulsa.edu). His research interests include consumer behavior issues that focus on life transitions, pricing, and e-commerce.

David J. Glew, PhD, is Assistant Professor of Management, University of North Carolina, 601 South College Road, Wilmington, NC 28403-5969 (E-mail: glewj@uncw.edu). His research interests include person-environment fit, work teams, and personal values.

Marc D. Street, PhD, is Assistant Professor of Management, University of South Florida, College of Business, 140 7th Avenue South, St. Petersburg, FL 33701 (E-mail: mdstreetdr@hotmail.com). His research interests include ethical decision making and human resource management.

The first author would like to thank the research office at the University of Missouri for providing financial support for this study. The authors express their thanks to the guest editor and the anonymous reviewers for their helpful comments on an earlier version of this article.

[Haworth co-indexing entry note]: "The Genesis of Relationships: Boundary Spanners' Appraisals of the Career Entry Transition." Wood, Charles M., David J. Glew, and Marc D. Street. Co-published simultaneously in *Journal of Relationship Marketing* (Best Business Books, an imprint of The Haworth Press, Inc.) Vol. 3, No. 2/3, 2004, pp. 5-24; and: *Internal Relationship Management: Linking Human Resources to Marketing Performance* (ed: Michael D. Hartline, and David Bejou) Best Business Books, an imprint of The Haworth Press, Inc., 2004, pp. 5-24. Single or multiple copies of this article are available for a fee from The Haworth Document Delivery Service [1-800-HAWORTH, 9:00 a.m. - 5:00 p.m. (EST). E-mail address: docdelivery@haworthpress.com].

5

SUMMARY. Productive relationships between a company and its customers are often the result of positive relationships between the company and its boundary spanning employees. The career entry transition marks the beginning of these interpersonal relationships, which have a significant impact on marketing performance. Using a sample of newly hired boundary spanning employees, we examine the influence of individual difference factors on boundary spanners' appraisals of the career entry transition. Significant relationships are found between boundary spanners' positive and negative appraisals of the transition and personal and non-organizational factors: perceived centrality of the work role, availability of resources (finances, social support, personal hope), and sense of coherence. *[Article copies available for a fee from The Haworth Document Delivery Service: 1-800-HAWORTH. E-mail address: <docdelivery@ haworthpress.com> Website: <http://www.HaworthPress.com> © 2004 by The Haworth Press, Inc. All rights reserved.]*

KEYWORDS. Boundary spanners, career entry, transition, appraisal

Practicing marketing managers and scholars alike have long known that an important determinant of the nature of the employer-employee relationship is the employee's perceptions of the quality of his or her experience during the initial phases of the employment process (Jones & George 1998; Johnston et al. 1990). In the management literature, the study of this particular aspect of the employment process has been conducted primarily by human resource management (HRM) scholars. Traditionally, these scholars have viewed the quality of the employee entry transition process as affected by three distinct human resource functions: pre-entry activities such as the interview process; awareness and acceptance of the firm's expectations, norms, and culture provided by orientation activities; and the development and maintenance of relevant skills and knowledge provided by training and development initiatives (Mathis & Jackson 2001).

In terms of the above HRM functions, scholars have been successful in establishing empirical support for a link between each function and organizationally desirable outcomes. For example, realistic job previews–a type of interview designed to give potential employees a realistic picture of the job in question and the context in which it is performed–have been shown to result in lower levels of turnover (Philips 1998). Effective orientation programs help create favorable impressions of the organization and increase the likelihood of new employees being favorably accepted by existing coworkers (Nelson & Quick 1991). Additionally, strong orientation programs have been shown to be predictive of high levels of organizational commitment, high levels of job satisfaction, and low levels of absenteeism (Mathis & Jackson 2001). Finally, HRM scholars have established numerous important benefits of training and development programs. Such programs facilitate a more comprehensive career transition experience by employees. Among the benefits accruing from training and development programs are increases in productivity, reduction in errors, lower levels of turnover, and a reduction in the amount of required employee supervision (Mathis & Jackson 2001). In sum, then, it appears that the entry transition experience is a crucial antecedent factor for marketing performance, and several other important organizational outcomes; namely, stronger organizational commitment, higher job satisfaction, lower turnover, and increased productivity.

Although HRM scholars have established the importance of HRM functions on the entry transition experience, to date, the majority of research in this area has focused on organizational-level variables and their impact on employee appraisals of the transition experience. In contrast, relatively little research attention has been directed at understanding the potential influence of individual-level variables on employee perceptions of the entry transition process. Considering such factors will help complete our understanding of those elements that affect employees' entry transition experiences. For instance, the amount of social support–from external sources (family, friends) and internal work sources (peers)–an individual receives during the entry transition period will likely affect his or her evaluation of the transition experience. The purpose of this paper is to consider such individual-level variables and their impact on employees' perceptions and appraisals of the entry process. Specifically, this paper takes a broader view of the transition process by focusing on the career entry experience from the employee's perspective and by considering the influence of personal and non-organizational factors on subsequent appraisals of the transition.

In this examination of the career entry experience, particular attention is given to boundary spanners–marketing personnel that develop and monitor relationships with important constituents outside the organization. In short, these employees represent the organization in interactions with key stakeholders. As noted earlier, entry transition experiences have been shown to be predictive of subsequent levels of key attitudes, such as job satisfaction and organizational commitment.

A successful entry transition experience is especially important with regard to boundary spanners, since outcomes such as job satisfaction have been shown to have clear links with the satisfaction and loyalty of customers (cf. Griffith 2001). Understanding the factors that influence boundary spanners' appraisals of their entry transition experiences will benefit marketing scholars and practicing HR managers alike.

In the sections that follow, the impact of several individual-level variables on boundary spanners' assessments of their entrance into organizations is examined. First, a literature review and discussion of the variables used in the study is presented. In doing so, research findings in psychology, marketing, and management are drawn upon to advance hypotheses regarding the key factors that contribute to excellent entrance experiences. These hypotheses are then tested using data obtained from new hires in boundary spanning positions across a variety of industries. The paper concludes with a discussion of the results and summary of the contributions this paper makes to the marketing literature.

LITERATURE REVIEW

The boundary spanning function encompasses the activities of employees who develop and manage relationships with customers and other key outside parties (Griffin 2002). Examples include salespeople, industrial buyers, public relations representatives, service providers, customer service employees, top management, and marketing managers. For most companies, the actions, attitudes, and behaviors of their boundary spanning personnel are absolutely crucial to their success. Crosby and Evans (1990) argued that customers often have a stronger relationship with a company's representatives than with the company itself, and that the quality of relationships developed with customers is an important antecedent to a company's long-term success. Because a boundary spanner is often the primary contact point with customers, his or her attitudes about the company play an important role in the customers' satisfaction with and loyalty to the organization.

Although management and industrial/organizational psychology scholars have established that a strong causal link from job satisfaction to performance does not exist at the individual employee level (Iaffaldano & Muchinsky 1992), individual job satisfaction does significantly affect other key behaviors and attitudes. For instance, in a study of field salespeople, Babakus et al. (1999) found significant relationships between satisfaction and increased organizational commitment, and between satisfaction and decreased intentions to leave the organization. Satisfaction also influences behaviors and attitudes such as job involvement, absenteeism, and organizational citizenship or "helping" behaviors (Griffin 2002). In addition, some evidence suggests the average level of individual-level satisfaction among an organization's employees influences organizational-level outcomes, including company performance (Ostroff 1992). In sum, when employees feel good about their jobs, they are more likely to hold attitudes and engage in behaviors that will be beneficial to the organization. When those employees are boundary spanners operating in a marketing function, they are more likely to exhibit a range of behaviors that build strong positive relationships with customers. This gives incentive for managers to carefully cultivate the relationship between a company and its boundary spanning employees from the very beginning. Doing so requires an understanding of the career entry transition from the employee's perspective (Johnston et al. 1990).

Career Entry Transitions

Transitions take many forms across a person's lifespan. According to Cowan (1991), the root meaning of transition is derived from two Latin words meaning "to go across." Examples of major life transitions include marriage, career entry, new parenthood, divorce, and retirement. During transitions old cognitive/affective structures and behavior patterns are reorganized and new patterns are developed. According to Upcraft (1989), individuals in the midst of transitions attempt to accomplish two primary objectives: adapt to the demands of the new life state and bring the emotional elements temporarily associated with the transition under control by integrating them into ongoing decisions and behaviors. The process of leaving college life and taking on a work career is a major life transition and is often accompanied by a strong affective experience and substantial changes in individuals' perceptions of control and well-being. For example, Munton and West (1995) suggested that up to 50 percent of all relocation transitions have a significant negative effect on the subjective psychological well-being of employees and their families.

The concept of individual roles is central to our study of the appraisal process. Building on previous work by Biddle (1979) and Allen and van de Vliert (1982), we use the term "role" to refer to a set of behaviors associated with a person's position in a social system that has individualized meaning and is guided by societal assumptions and norms. A "role transition" is defined as the relatively permanent change by a person from one set of expected positional behaviors to another at role entry or exit, or when the expected behaviors associated with an existing role are drastically changed (Allen & van de Vliert 1982). Like other major life events, the career entry transition for new boundary spanners involves multiple role transitions (e.g., exiting college roles, moving geographically, losing friends but gaining others; Wanous 1992).

Career entry transitions are significant and costly events for companies as well as for boundary spanners. Companies work hard to find and keep quality employees. Employee turnover results in major costs to companies for hiring, training, and the period of adjustment (usually several months) when replacement employees are not yet productive (Futrell & Parasuraman 1984; Johnston et al. 1990). Unfortunately, employee turnover rates are at their highest among newly hired employees (Wanous 1992). If an organization can better manage the transition event for new employees, it is likely they will be able to reduce these costs.

If marketing boundary spanners have a negative transition experience, the costs to the organization may be substantial because of the critical relationships customers have with these company representatives. These costs go beyond the expense of finding and hiring a new employee and include losses from forgone sales, depleted goodwill, and spoiled relationships. Therefore, an examination of the entry transition process and the factors that may help companies have more successful entrances of new hires is warranted.

Appraisals of the Transition Process

Research in psychology has revealed that when people are confronted with a new or unusual circumstance, one of the dominant reactive cognitive functions employed is "appraisal." Appraisal has been defined as an evaluative process that determines why and to what extent a particular transaction between a person and his/her environment is benign, beneficial, and/or harmful (Lazarus & Folkman 1984). Mere knowledge that a transition has occurred does not yield insight into the complexity or meaning of the transition to the individual. Indeed, two people entering a company at the same time will experience and appraise the transition very differently depending on a complex interplay of personal, organizational, and non-organizational factors (e.g., Mowday, Porter & Steers 1982). Various factors related to transitions have been validated in research involving boundary spanners (Churchill et al. 1985; Singh 1998; Johnston et al. 1990). Lazarus and Folkman (1984) assert that the outcome of the appraisal process is the key to understanding an individual's response to the event and subsequent behavior. Thus, our focus is on understanding the factors that influence the appraisal process.

More specifically, we focus on boundary spanners' appraisals of their career entry transitions (i.e., the transition experience of newly hired employees). Previous research has established that the initial attitudes and perceptions of employees at the earliest phases of their careers strongly predict their future performance and turnover intentions (Buchanan 1974; Johnston et al. 1990). In a similar vein, Hrebiniak and Alutto (1972) found that the *anticipation* of trust among new employees leads to the later formation of attitudes such as organizational commitment. Because new hires have no history upon which they can evaluate the strength or quality of their relationship with a company, it is likely that their appraisals of the transition process into the company will have an important influence on later levels of trust, productivity, and organizational commitment.

We take a holistic perspective of career entry to boundary spanner positions, and view the taking on of a new career as a major life event for an individual on the same order as getting married, having a first child, or retiring. Certainly a company's training and orientation efforts help employees adapt to that particular organization, but the appraisal process begins much earlier, beginning with their assessment of the first point of contact with the company, extending through the interviewing and hiring decision, and continuing during the actual transition into a role with the company. In addition, the appraisal is not only influenced by organizational factors, but also most likely by a number of personal and non-organizational factors that operate on an individual during the entry transition. This is a component of the appraisal process that has traditionally been understudied.

Particularly for new employees, non-organizational influences on the appraisal process and subsequent outcomes include factors such as personal attitudes toward the work role, changes in the availability of time, financial, and social support resources for the person, the presence of other life events occurring at the same time, and individual difference variables such as sense of coherence. Operating apart from organizational factors, it is quite likely that these factors will alter the employee's appraisal of the transition process, and in turn influence the employee's morale, commitment, and tenure with the company. In addition, traditional measures of organization- and non-organization factors are often designed for current employees. In contrast, our interest is in newly hired employees.

Finally, we note an important aspect of entry process appraisals that is sometimes overlooked. Boundary spanners may have strong positive appraisals about certain parts of their transition (e.g., increased pay, status, and responsibility), and at the same time have strong negative appraisals about other parts of the transition (e.g., relocation, travel away from family, increased pressure and stress). If HR managers are to fully understand boundary spanners' appraisals, they must recognize both dimensions of the employee's evaluation.

HYPOTHESES

Because a boundary spanner's new role lies at the heart of the transition process, we first examine how perceptions of role centrality affect the transition process. A role is considered central to a person if it is strongly defended by the person, is bolstered by beliefs and values, and affects a wide range of the person's behaviors (Biddle 1979). For example, a new boundary spanner who has begun a job in a company that espouses values consistent with his or her own will experience greater role centrality. In contrast, a new boundary spanner who has accepted new employment simply as a means to a different end (e.g., paying the rent) will experience lower role centrality. Roles perceived to be more central to a person's self-definition will tend to be sought after, and entry to such roles is predicted to yield positive appraisals of the transition. In contrast, roles perceived as less central to a person's self-definition are likely to be enacted with little zest, and at times reluctantly, resulting in a negative appraisal of the transition. As mentioned above, we predict an impact on both positive and negative elements of the appraisal:

H_{1a}: Boundary spanners' perceptions of the centrality of their work roles will *increase* the *positive* appraisal of their career entry transition process.

H_{1b}: Boundary spanners' perceptions of the centrality of their work roles will *decrease* the *negative* appraisal of their career entry transition process.

Next, we predict the available resources a boundary spanner has will influence the appraisal process. Depending on the conditions under which the transition occurs, the transition may have different effects (George 1993). For example, boundary spanners who have access to resources that allow them to effectively cope with the stress that accompanies transitions (Goolsby 1992) will likely evaluate the transition more positively.

Stryker and Statham (1985) point out that under some circumstances, adding a new role to an existing role set can *add* important resources and flexibility, thereby reducing rather than increasing strain. For example, when new employees take on boundary spanning roles, increases in finances, social support at work, and a personal sense of hope about the future are likely to help mitigate the negative changes (Hunt, Chonko & Wood 1985) accompanying the transition (e.g., reduced free time, increased time away from home). We examine the effect of five potential resources, and predict that each will influence boundary spanners' appraisals of the transition process:

H_{2a}: Boundary spanners' perceptions of the availability of resources (time, finances, social support from friends and family, and personal hope) will *increase* the *positive* appraisal of their career entry transition process.

H_{2b}: Boundary spanners' perceptions of the availability of resources (time, finances, social support from friends and family, and personal hope) will *decrease* the *negative* appraisal of their career entry transition process.

Sense of coherence (SOC) is a multi-dimensional individual difference characteristic that acts as a buffer, or resistor, to the experience of role stress (Antonovsky 1979, 1993). There are three primary dimensions of sense of coherence. *Comprehensibility* is described as "the extent to which one perceives the stimuli that confront one . . . as information that is ordered, consistent, structured, and clear, rather than noise-chaotic, disordered, random, accidental, inexplicable" (Antonovsky 1979: 16-17). *Manageability* is the "extent to which . . . resources are at one's disposal which are adequate to meet the demands posed by the stimuli that bombard one" (Antonovsky 1979: 17). Finally, *meaningfulness* "refers to the extent to which . . . at least some of the problems and demands posed by living are worth investing energy in, are worthy of commitment and engagement, are challenges that are "welcome" rather than burdens . . ." (Antonovsky 1979: 18). According to Antonovsky, theory and research findings have established that these three components are "inextricably intertwined" (1979: 19) and that, all things equal, high levels in one aspect will result in high levels of SOC overall. Further, high levels of SOC imply that the individual is in a position to manage stressful situations more effectively than an individual low in SOC. Indeed, the high-level SOC employee is much less likely to perceive the stimuli as stressful in the first place.

Entry transitions that are perceived as being non-stressful are likely to be evaluated in positive terms. In contrast, highly stressful transitions are likely to be viewed negatively. Since individuals with high SOC are less likely to report (or even experience) the effects of work-induced stress than are low SOC workers, it stands to reason that high SOC employees will evaluate their career entry transition process more positively, and less negatively, than will low SOC employees. Therefore, we propose:

H_{3a}: Boundary spanners' sense of coherence will *increase* the *positive* appraisal of their career entry transition process.

H_{3b}: Boundary spanners' sense of coherence will *decrease* the *negative* appraisal of their career entry transition process.

METHODS

Sample and Procedure

Boundary spanners (N = 104) from a variety of industries were included in the study subject to two constraints: (1) they were ages 20-26, and (2) they had been working full-time nine months or less since graduation from a four-year college. These constraints allowed us to focus on recent, early post-college employment transitions. Recruiting subjects who met the requirements for the study was accomplished using alumni and career placement lists obtained from a Midwestern university and by requesting help from mid-sized companies in nearby metropolitan areas. The seven companies that participated were located in two states and represented major telecommunications, insurance, manufacturing, accounting, and retail firms. The final sample included employees engaged in a variety of boundary spanning functions: marketing, sales, corporate relations, and customer service.

Questionnaires were administered in person by the researchers to employees during lunch breaks in conference or seminar rooms under similar controlled conditions. Fourteen sessions were conducted in 11 locations. The questionnaire took approximately 45 minutes to complete, and each participant was paid $10 at the close of the session. As an added incentive, participants were given the opportunity to be entered in a drawing for one of five $100 gift certificates good at any store in their regional mall.

Measures

Appraisal. Appraisal was conceptualized as two unipolar constructs rather than as a single bipolar construct in order to assess the nature of positive and negative appraisals. This approach is consistent with previous research on the nature of affective states which asserts that positive and negative affect are independent constructs and should be assessed separately (Warr, Barter, & Brownbridge 1983). The measures of positive and negative appraisal were constructed using a combination of appraisal measures used in previous research (Fish 1986; Stone & Neal 1984). An initial appraisal instrument consisting of 20 items (11 positive and 9 negative; all anchored by "Strongly Agree" and "Strongly Disagree") was pre-tested with a convenience sample of student subjects who were asked to report their attitudes toward their upcoming entry into their career.

To verify that the positive and negative appraisal measures represented two distinct constructs (and were not merely opposites of the same construct), the 20 items were entered into a principal components factor analysis with a varimax rotation. Two factors emerged, both with eigenvalues greater than one. In addition, the skree plot strongly suggested retaining two separate factors. The internal consistency of each set of items was then examined. The reliability estimate of the 11-item positive appraisal measure was high (Cronbach's $\alpha = .93$), and the reliability estimate of the negative appraisal measure was acceptable ($\alpha = .73$).

Role Centrality. To determine each respondent's perceptions of the centrality of both their college role and their career role, a scale was developed from existing measures of attitude toward objects and attitude toward acts (Batra & Ray 1986; Maheswaren & Meyers-Levy 1990). Items were carefully selected based on their face validity and their appropriateness for the study sample. Participants were asked: "Please think for a moment about how you feel about working in your current job, and then indicate to what degree the following items reflect those attitudes and feelings." The eight items were: Meaningful, Relevant, Central, Essential, Valuable, Matters to me, Of concern to me, and Important to me. Respondents indicated answers on 7-point scales anchored by "Not at all" and "Very Much." The eight-item measure demonstrated high internal consistency for role entry (into career; $\alpha = .94$) as well as for role exit (from college; $\alpha = .90$).

Resources. Participants were given the following instructions: "Please indicate how you feel today about how available the following resources are to you." The availability of five key resources was measured: time, finances, social support (friends, family), and personal hope (Kobasa & Pucetti 1983; Luborsky et al. 1973; Stone & Neal 1984). Five 7-point scale items anchored by "I have little available" and "I have plenty available" were used to assess these resources.

Sense of Coherence. Antonovsky developed the Sense of Coherence (SOC) scale which has shown good reliability (high internal consistency and test-retest correlations) and convergent and discriminant validity (e.g., Antonovsky 1993). Sample items include: "Until now your life has had: No clear goals or purpose/Very clear goals and purpose"; and "Doing the things you do every day is: A source of deep pleasure and satisfaction/A source of pain and boredom." In the current study the scale demonstrated acceptable reliability ($\alpha = .78$).

Other Life Transitions. The presence of other life transitions may interfere with results obtained from examining the career entry transition. Therefore, the incidence of other transitions occurring within the last six months was measured and included as a control variable. This variable was assessed using the top twenty-five life event items from the inventory developed by Holmes and Rahe (1967) and Dohrenwend and Dohrenwend (1974). Respondents were asked if any of the twenty-five events (e.g., divorce, gain of a new family member, foreclosure of mortgage or loan, outstanding personal achievement) had occurred in the past six months, and if so, the perceived personal impact of the event. These items were measured on a five-point scale anchored by "Little impact" and "Great impact." A score for this scale was calculated and used as a control variable in the analysis.

ANALYSIS

Hypothesis 1a predicted that positive appraisals of a transition would be influenced by role centrality. Multiple regression analysis was conducted to test this prediction. In order to control for the possible influence of other major life events within the past six months and the centrality of the employee's prior college role, measures of these constructs were included in the analysis as control variables. As predicted, entering a highly valued and central work role is positively and significantly associated with positive appraisals of transitions into these roles. Hypothesis 1b predicted that appraisals of a transition would be more negative as the perceived centrality of the new role declined. The overall model is not significant, and therefore does not support this hypothesis. These results are presented in Table 1.

Hypothesis 2a predicted the extent to which the availability of five resources would increase the employee's positive appraisals of the transition. Hypothesis 2b stated that available resources would reduce an employee's negative appraisals. As predicted, personal hope significantly increased positive appraisals of the transition process; however, it did not reduce negative appraisals. As expected, the availability of financial resources reduced negative appraisals; but it did not increase

TABLE 1. The Effect of Role Centrality on Boundary Spanner Appraisals of Career Entry Transitions

	Positive Appraisals			Negative Appraisals		
	df	*Parameter Estimate*	*t-value*	*df*	*Parameter Estimate*	*t-value*
Presence of Other Life Events	1	0.27	1.97[a]	---	---	---
Work Role Centrality	1	0.78	12.45[b]	1	−0.01	−0.12
College Role Centrality	1	−0.03	−0.34	1	−0.14	−1.51
Source of Variation	*df*	*Sum of Squares*		*df*	*Sum of Squares*	
Model	3	89.70		2	1.91	
Error	100	54.95		101	81.47	
Total	103	144.65		103	83.38	
	F = 54.41 (p < .0001)			F = 1.18 (p < .31)		
	$R^2 = 0.62$			$R^2 = 0.02$		

[a] $p < 0.10$ [b] $p < 0.001$

positive appraisals. Time resources and social support from family did not influence positive or negative appraisals. Social support from friends did not reduce negative appraisals, and showed an unexpected negative relationship with positive appraisals. These results, presented in Table 2, provide partial support for Hypotheses 2a and 2b.

A boundary spanner's sense of coherence is also predicted to influence appraisals of the transition process. Although the conceptual underpinnings of sense of coherence are different than they are for the five resources discussed above, to maintain simultaneous controls among the variables, sense of coherence was included in the same analyses as were the five aforementioned resources. This approach also reduces the increased probability of type II errors resulting from conducting multiple tests. Thus, the results for the tests of Hypotheses 3a and 3b are also shown in Table 2. As predicted by H_{3a}, a boundary spanner's sense of coherence does increase his or her positive appraisal of the transition process. Also, as predicted by H_{3b}, sense of coherence reduces the negative appraisal of the transition process.

TABLE 2. The Effect of Resource Availability on Boundary Spanner Appraisals of Career Entry Transitions

	Positive Appraisals			Negative Appraisals		
	df	Parameter Estimate	t-value	df	Parameter Estimate	t-value
Sense of Coherence	1	0.54	3.69[c]	1	−0.26	−2.23[a]
Time Resources	1	0.02	0.43	1	−0.03	−0.73
Financial Resources	1	0.02	0.34	1	−0.12	−2.75[b]
Social Support Resources–Friends	1	−0.16	−2.47[a]	1	0.03	0.54
Social Support Resources–Family	1	0.06	0.68	1	−0.03	−0.41
Personal Hope Resources	1	0.28	2.98[b]	1	−0.00	−0.04
Source of Variation	df	Sum of Squares		df	Sum of Squares	
Model	6	39.25		6	12.85	
Error	97	105.40		97	70.53	
Total	103	144.65		103	83.38	
	F = 6.02 (p < .0001)			F = 2.95 (p < .011)		
	R^2 = 0.27			R^2 = 0.15		

[a]p < 0.05   [b]p < 0.01   [c]p < 0.001

DISCUSSION

Boundary spanners fill a critical marketing role in organizations. Their attitudes and behaviors have implications for the strength of customer relationships, the image of the organization, and the financial viability of the company. Prior research has documented numerous benefits arising from employees' positive evaluations of the organization. Most notably, empirical evidence exists that employee satisfaction is related to customer satisfaction and loyalty (Griffith 2001). In this study, we examined factors that influence boundary spanners' appraisals of the transition into the organization. To the extent that boundary spanners' appraisals are positive, these desired marketing outcomes may be expected.

In this study, we found that the centrality of boundary spanners' work roles increased their positive appraisals of the transition process, but did not decrease their negative evaluations of this process. This pair of findings may at first seem counterintuitive, but it lends support to the idea that positive and negative appraisals are separate constructs. In a classic study of employee motivation, Herzberg (1959) discovered that certain organizational factors mainly influenced job satisfaction while others primarily influenced job dissatisfaction. Role centrality may simply be a factor that influences positive appraisals of the transition process, but does not influence negative appraisals. Another possible explanation is that at least some negative aspects of the transition are to be expected. In other words, the transition involves "sunk costs" that the employee is willing to endure to secure employment. Role centrality, although it would increase the positive appraisal of the transition, would be unable to eliminate, or even reduce, these expected negative aspects (even when role centrality is extremely high). In any case, HRM and marketing managers should be aware that role centrality plays an important role in boundary spanners' evaluations as they enter the company. Based on our findings, managers who are able to enhance the perceived centrality of boundary spanners' roles during the transition process may increase the desired outcomes associated with positive appraisals.

Two of the five personal resources examined in the study influenced boundary spanners' appraisals as expected: personal hope increased positive evaluations and financial resources decreased negative evaluations. These findings provide some support for our basic argument that non-organizational factors play a role in the evaluations boundary spanners make as they enter the organization. Personal hope may have allowed boundary spanners to focus on the positive aspects of the new role despite the stress and strain associated with the transition process. Similarly, financial resources may have "buffered" boundary spanners from the negative facets of role transition. The total number of such resources available to the boundary spanner could potentially make a vast difference in his or her entry experience. Although personal resources are often beyond the control of organizational influences, managers may benefit from simply understanding the effects of personal resources, and potentially could make adjustments when the stress associated with entry transition overwhelms the personal resources available to new employees.

Unexpectedly, one personal resource, social support from friends, significantly reduced the positive appraisals boundary spanners make of the transition process. The reason for this is not entirely clear, but one explanation may be that the transition itself jeopardizes continued social support from friends. A new job with increased responsibilities, potentially in a new location, might impinge on existing social ties. Given that the sample of boundary spanners who participated in this study were recent college graduates, it may be that they have a strong circle of friends, but are unable to benefit from it, given the demands of the job. Social support from friends did not significantly increase negative appraisals, but the coefficient was positive.

Of all the variables included in the study, boundary spanners' sense of coherence had the strongest impact on transition appraisals. As predicted, sense of coherence significantly increased the level of positive appraisals and significantly decreased the level of negative appraisals. These results suggest at least two implications for HRM and marketing managers. First, anything that can be done to increase boundary spanners' sense of coherence as they complete the transition is likely to improve their appraisal of the process. For example, since we know that an important dimension of SOC is the extent to which the individual feels that he or she has the necessary resources to meet the demands of their new role (e.g., the manageability dimension), management would be wise to ensure that all new boundary spanners enter a work environment characterized by access to the type and quantity of resources needed to make the transition as smooth as possible.

Second, organizations may find it worthwhile to screen new applicants for boundary spanning positions based on their sense of coherence. Screening specifically designed to identify individuals' high in the meaningfulness aspect of SOC is likely to prove fruitful since these individuals tend to view stressful situations in a more positive light than do individuals who exhibit lower scores on this dimension. Indeed, these relatively stress-resilient employees will see such situations as challenges rather than burdens. Thus, use of the SOC scale might very well represent a valuable addition to the HR manager's collection of selection tools. Again, this is important because ultimately, the effects of employee attitudes will be displayed in enhanced or reduced marketing performance.

LIMITATIONS AND FUTURE RESEARCH

Our results provide a glimpse at several factors that influence internal relationship management. Certainly other factors play a critical role in this process. Importantly, however, this study examined personal and non-organizational factors of a key set of organizational employees. Understanding the transition process of boundary spanners may help HRM and marketing managers avoid the consequences of negative transitions (e.g., turnover, dissatisfaction) and take advantage of the benefits of positive transitions (e.g., organizational commitment, employee satisfaction, customer satisfaction and loyalty).

Of course, our study is not without limitations. We examine the transition experience of a relatively specialized sample–recent college graduates in their early careers. This sample allows us to identify important aspects of the entry transition appraisal, but it does not allow us to generalize our findings to other types of employees, such as mid- and late-career boundary spanners who are moving to new jobs between companies or even within the same company. Another limitation to our findings is that we collected subjects' subjective perceptions of the various measures. Ideally, we would have assessed objective outcomes as well, such as performance and other visible behaviors. These outcomes would have been difficult to obtain, but more important, they may not have provided reliable information in our current sample. For example, assessing the performance of new employees as they climb the learning curve in their new jobs would likely produce a relatively unstable measure. Including this information would be more appropriate once performance levels stabilize.

In conclusion, we recommend three basic directions for future research. First, in contrast to prior research on the effects of transition appraisals, our study examined exclusively non-organizational factors. Therefore, future research that combines both organizational and non-organizational factors will help explain the relative influence of each set. Second, the permanence of the beneficial effects of positive transitions should be examined. Previous research has revealed that for salespeople, there is a curvilinear relationship between time in a work role and overall job satisfaction, with the most satisfied salespeople being those who have held their jobs for two years or less (Churchill et al. 1985). It may be that the benefits of positive transitions expire over time. A more complete study of boundary spanners at pre-entry, early employment, and later career phases would help answer this question. One strategy to pursue this goal is to follow the same employees longitudinally through these stages. Finally, we recommend the examination and development of institutional efforts, such as recruiting, selection and orientation programs, that are designed specifically to increase the likelihood of positive appraisals by key marketing personnel.

REFERENCES

Allen, Vernon L. and Evert van de Vliert (1982), "A Role Theoretical Perspective on Transitional Processes," in *Role Transitions: Explorations and Explanations*, (eds. Vernon L. Allen and Evert van de Vliert), New York: Plenum Press.

Antonovsky, Aaron (1979), *Health, Stress, and Coping*, San Francisco: Jossey-Bass Publishers.

Antonovsky, Aaron (1993), "The Structure and Properties of the Sense of Coherence Scale," *Social Science and Medicine, 36* (March): 725-733.

Babakus, Emin, David W. Cravens, Mark Johnston, and William C. Moncrief (1999), "The Role of Emotional Exhaustion in Sales Force Attitude and Behavior Relationships," *Journal of the Academy of Marketing Science, 27* (1): 58-70.

Batra, Rajeev and Michael L. Ray (1986), "Affective Responses Mediating Acceptance of Advertising," *Journal of Consumer Research, 13* (September): 234-249.

Biddle, Bruce J. (1979), *Role Theory: Expectations, Identities, and Behaviors*, New York: Academic Press.

Buchanan, Bruce (1974), "Building Organizational Commitment: The Socialization of Managers in Work Organizations," *Administrative Science Quarterly, 19* (December): 533-546.

Churchill, Gilbert A., Jr., Neil M. Ford, Steven W. Hartley, and Orville C. Walker, Jr. (1985), "The Determinants of Salesperson Performance: A Meta-Analysis," *Journal of Marketing Research, 22* (May): 103-118.

Cowan, Philip A. (1991), "Individual and Family Life Transitions: A Proposal for a New Definition," in *Family Transitions*, Philip A. Cowan and Mavis Hetherington (eds.); Hillsdale, NJ: Lawrence Erlbaum Associates, Publishers.

Crosby, Lawrence A. and Kenneth R. Evans (1990), "Relationship Quality in Services Selling: An Interpersonal Influence Perspective," *Journal of Marketing, 54* (July): 68-81.

Dohrenwend, Bruce P. and Barbara Snell Dohrenwend (1974), *Stressful Life Events: Their Nature and Effects*, New York: John Wiley and Sons.

Fish, Thomas A. (1986), "Semantic Differential Assessment of Benign, Threat, and Challenge Appraisals of Life Events," *Canadian Journal of Behavioral Science, 18* (January): 1-13.

Futrell, Charles M. and A. Parasuraman (1984), "The Relationship of Satisfaction and Performance to Salesforce Turnover," *Journal of Marketing, 48* (Fall): 33-40.

George (1993), "Sociological Perspectives on Life Transitions," *American Review of Sociology, 19*: 353-373.

Goolsby, Jerry R. (1992), "A Theory of Role Stress in Boundary Spanning Positions of Marketing Organizations," *Journal of the Academy of Marketing Science, 20* (Spring): 155-164.

Griffin, Ricky (2002), *Management* (7th ed.). Houghton Mifflin Company: New York.

Griffith, J. (2001), "Do Satisfied Employees Satisfy Customers? Support-Services Staff Morale and Satisfaction Among Public School Administrators, Students, and Parents," *Journal of Applied Social Psychology*: 1627-1658.

Herzberg, F., B. Mausner, and B. Snyderman (1959), *The Motivation to Work*. New York: Wiley.

Holmes, Thomas H. and Richard H. Rahe (1967), "The Social Readjustment Rating Scale," *Journal of Psychosomatic Research, 11*: 213-218.

Hrebiniak, Lawrence and Joseph A. Alutto (1972), "Personal and Role-related Factors in the Development of Organizational Commitment," *Administrative Science Quarterly, 17* (3): 555-572.

Hunt, Shelby D., Lawrence B. Chonko, and Van R. Wood (1985), "Organizational Commitment and Marketing," *Journal of Marketing, 49* (Winter): 112-126.

Iaffaldano, M. T., and P. M. Muchinsky (1992), Job satisfaction and job performance: A meta-analysis. *Psychological Bulletin, 97:* 251-273.

Johnston, Mark W., A. Parasuraman, Charles M. Futrell, and William C. Black (1990), "A Longitudinal Assessment of the Impact of Selected Organizational Influences on Salespeople's Organizational Commitment During Early Employment," *Journal of Marketing Research, 27* (August): 333-344.

Jones, Gareth R. and Jennifer M. George (1998), "The Experience and Evolution of Trust: Implications for Cooperation and Teamwork," *Academy of Management Review, 23* (July): 531-546.

Kobasa, Suzanne C. Ouellette and Mark C. Puccetti (1983), "Personality and Social Resources in Stress Resistance," *Journal of Personality and Social Psychology, 45* (October): 839-850.

Lazarus, Richard and Susan Folkman (1984), *Stress, Appraisal, and Coping*, New York: Springer Publishing Co.

Luborsky, L., T. C. Todd, and A. H. Katcher (1973), "A Self-Administered Social Assets Scale for Predicting Physical and Psychological Illness and Health," *Journal of Psychosomatic Research, 17*: 109-120.

Maheswaran, Durairja and Joan Meyers-Levy (1990), "The Influence of Message Framing and Issue Involvement," *Journal of Marketing Research, 27* (August): 361-367.

Mathis, R. L. and J. H. Jackson (2001), *Human Resource Management*. West Publishing Corporation: Minneapolis/St. Paul.

Mowday, Richard, Lyman W. Porter, and Richard M. Steers (1982), *Employee-Organizational Linkages: The Psychology of Commitment, Absenteeism, and Turnover*, San Francisco, CA: Academic Press, Inc.

Munton, Anthony G. and Michael A. West (1995), "Innovations and Personal Change: Patterns of Adjustment to Relocation," *Journal of Organizational Behavior, 16* (July): 363-375.

Nelson, D. and J. Quick (1991), "Social Support and Newcomer Adjustment in Organizations," *Journal of Organizational Behavior, 12*: 543-554.

Ostroff, C. (1992), "The Relationship between Satisfaction, Attitudes, and Performance: An Organizational-level Analysis," *Journal of Applied Psychology, 77*: 963-974.

Philips, Jean M. (1998), "Effects of Realistic Job Previews on Multiple Organizational Outcomes," *Academy of Management Journal, 41*: 673-690.

Singh, Jagdip (1998), "Striking a Balance in Boundary-Spanning Positions: An Investigation of Some Unconventional Influences of Role Stressors and Job Characteristic on Job Outcomes of Salespeople," *Journal of Marketing, 62* (July): 69-86.

Stone, Arthur and John M. Neale (1984), "New Measure of Daily Coping: Development and Preliminary Results," *Journal of Personality and Social Psychology, 46* (April): 892-906.

Stryker, Sheldon and Anne Statham (1985), "Symbolic Interaction and Role Theory," in *The Handbook of Social Psychology*: Volume 1, eds. Gardner Lindzey and Elliot Aronson; New York: Random House.

Upcraft, M. Lee (1989), "Understanding Student Development: Insights from Theory," in *The Freshman Year Experience: Helping Students Survive and Succeed in College*, eds. M. Lee Upcraft, John N. Gardner, and Associates; San Francisco, CA: Jossey-Bass Inc. Publishers.

Wanous, John P. (1992), *Organizational Entry: Recruitment, Selection, Orientation and Socialization of Newcomers*, Reading, MA: Addison-Wesley Publishing Co.

Warr, Peter, Joanna Barter, and Garry Brownbridge (1983), "On the Independence of Positive and Negative Affect," *Journal of Personality and Social Psychology, 44* (March): 644-651.

Individual Differences Among Service Employees: The Conundrum of Employee Recruitment, Selection, and Retention

Michael D. Hartline

Florida State University

Tom De Witt

Bowling Green State University

SUMMARY. To do an excellent job of managing external relationships, service firms must be prepared to do an excellent job of managing

Dr. Michael D. Hartline, PhD, is Associate Professor of Marketing, College of Business, Florida State University, Tallahassee, FL 32306-1110 (E-mail: mhartlin@cob.fsu.edu). His research interests include services marketing, managing customer-contact employees, and strategy implementation. Dr. Hartline's research has appeared in the *Journal of Marketing*, the *Journal of Business Research*, the *Journal of Services Marketing*, and others.

Tom De Witt, PhD, is Assistant Professor of Marketing, College of Business Administration, Bowling Green State University, Bowling Green, OH 43403 (E-mail: tdewitt@cba.bgsu.edu). His research interests include services marketing, with a particular focus on group dynamics and teamwork among customer-contact employees and its effect on service delivery. Dr. De Witt's research has appeared in the *Journal of Service Research*, the *Journal of Relationship Marketing*, and in several national and regional conference proceedings.

[Haworth co-indexing entry note]: "Individual Differences Among Service Employees: The Conundrum of Employee Recruitment, Selection, and Retention." Hartline, Michael D., and Tom De Witt. Co-published simultaneously in *Journal of Relationship Marketing* (Best Business Books, an imprint of The Haworth Press, Inc.) Vol. 3, No. 2/3, 2004, pp. 25-42; and: *Internal Relationship Management: Linking Human Resources to Marketing Performance* (ed: Michael D. Hartline, and David Bejou) Best Business Books, an imprint of The Haworth Press, Inc., 2004, pp. 25-42. Single or multiple copies of this article are available for a fee from The Haworth Document Delivery Service [1-800-HAWORTH, 9:00 a.m. - 5:00 p.m. (EST). E-mail address: docdelivery@haworthpress.com].

http://www.haworthpress.com/web/JRM
Digital Object Identifier: 10.1300/J366v03n02_03

internal relationships. This effort begins with recruiting, selecting, and retaining employees who are likely to serve customers well. While service firms strive to match the knowledge, ability, and skills of potential employees to the requirements of the job, most do not have the time or the resources to implement elaborate recruitment and selection systems. This is especially true among services where relatively high turnover levels mandate that recruitment and selection processes be fast and inexpensive. To meet this challenge, managers often focus on a set of easily identifiable individual characteristics, such as experience, job tenure, age, or education that can be assessed during the time of an interview or scan of a job application. This study examines the effect of these characteristics on the attitudes and responses of service employees that are critical for the effective delivery of quality service (job satisfaction, self-efficacy, role stress, organizational commitment). The results indicate that satisfied and committed service employees tend to be older, better educated, and possess a great deal of service experience. These employees also appear to be better able to handle the stress associated with service positions. These characteristics are atypical of the service industry, where employees tend to be younger, possess relatively little experience in any one industry, and are less educated. Implications for managing the recruitment, selection, and retention of service employees are offered, as are directions for future research. *[Article copies available for a fee from The Haworth Document Delivery Service: 1-800-HAWORTH. E-mail address: <docdelivery@haworthpress.com> Website: <http://www.HaworthPress. com> © 2004 by The Haworth Press, Inc. All rights reserved.]*

KEYWORDS. Individual differences, service employees, experience, job tenure, age, education, job satisfaction, self-efficacy, role stress, organizational commitment

A relative consensus within the literature supports the contention that the highest level of perceived service quality is delivered by service employees who are satisfied with their jobs, exhibit high levels of self-efficacy and commitment, and exhibit low levels of role stress (Hartline and Ferrell 1996; Schneider and Bowen 1985; Singh 2000). Within the employee-customer interface, satisfied, confident, and committed employees are likely to perform better than dissatisfied, apprehensive, and uncommitted employees during the service encounter; leading to enhanced customer perceptions of service quality (Hartline and Ferrell

1996). Consequently, if a service firm intends to deliver an outstanding level of service to its customers, then it must be prepared to do an excellent job in attracting, developing, motivating, and retaining service employees who are likely to exhibit these types of responses (Berry and Parasuraman 1992).

While service quality is arguably the most critical factor in a service firm's long-term success and survival, many firms suffer from poor service delivery because they fail at the outset to select the proper employees for service positions. While the goal of employee selection is aimed at choosing individuals who have the necessary qualifications to perform a particular job well (Anthony, Perrewe, and Kacmar 1993), firms differ with respect to the complexity of their selection systems. Some firms employ elaborate systems, which require potential employees to perform through a series of interviews or job-relevant tests to predict performance (Behling 1998; O'Hara, Boles, and Johnston 1991). Other firms focus on key employee characteristics that are easily identified from job applications and/or quick face-to-face interviews.

While elaborate selection systems can be quite useful in identifying employees who possess requisite skills and abilities (Behling 1998), they are impractical when selecting employees to work in many service settings. For service firms, the time and expense of implementing elaborate selection procedures is typically considered to be a poor investment. The relatively high levels of employee turnover that occur in these settings force service firms to fill positions swiftly and inexpensively by scanning job applications and holding brief interviews with potential candidates. Since it is impossible to obtain complete information about an applicant under these circumstances, managers must rely upon a set of easily identifiable individual characteristics, such as experience, job tenure, age, or education, that can be assessed during the time of an interview or scan of a job application.

The purpose of this study is to examine how these easily identifiable characteristics are related to the attitudes and responses of service employees that are critical for the effective delivery of quality service. Our goal in doing this study is to determine which individual characteristics are in fact associated with the employee attitudes and responses that service firms seek. Further, we expect that our findings will stimulate future research in this area, as well as more in-depth studies of employee recruitment, selection, and retention strategies.

The paucity of research regarding the recruitment and selection of service employees provides little guidance in conducting our study. Consequently, our study is exploratory in nature as we are hesitant to proffer hypotheses. In the sections that follow, we review the relevant literature that connects employee characteristics to the attitudes and responses they exhibit. Then, we report the results of an empirical study to examine the effects of experience, job tenure, age, and education on the critical employee responses of job satisfaction, self-efficacy, role stress, and organizational commitment. Finally, we conclude with managerial implications and directions for future research.

INDIVIDUAL DIFFERENCES AND EMPLOYEES' JOB-RELATED RESPONSES

If high levels of service quality are indeed delivered by employees who are satisfied with their jobs, exhibit high levels of self-efficacy, low levels of role stress, and strong commitment, then it behooves managers to select and hire individuals who are most likely to exhibit these responses. Given the nature of the service industry and the endemic level of turnover facing service firms, the typical employee is one who has little industry experience, has a relatively short tenure in any one job, and is relatively younger and less educated than employees in many other industries. These individual differences are easily identifiable during the selection process. The question remains, however, as to which characteristics are most indicative of an employee who will display the appropriate attitudinal and behavior responses that are sought by managers.

Individual Differences and Job Satisfaction

The relationships among individual differences and job satisfaction have been studied more extensively than other attitudes and responses examined in this study. Job satisfaction is composed of different work-related facets (supervision, pay, coworkers, policies, the work itself, etc.) with which an employee may be either satisfied or dissatisfied (Taber and Alliger 1995).

An employee's experience in a given industry is a function of the employee's personal career choices and the amount of time that is spent in a particular industry. Overall, previous studies have been supportive of a positive relationship between industry experience and job satisfaction (cf. Bilgic 1998). In a study of full-time university employees, Decker and Borgen (1993) found that work experience, education, and age were positively related to job satisfaction. Similar results were obtained in a study of employees in the Kuwait oil industry (Al-Ajmi 2001).

Despite the positive effects of industry experience, research indicates that job tenure has the opposite effect on job satisfaction. Job tenure is defined as the length of time an employee has worked for his or her current company (O'Hara et al. 1991). In a study of firefighters, Traut, Larsen, and Feimer (2000) found that employees with less time on the job were more positive about their organizations and that the most satisfied employees were in their earliest years of service. Researchers speculate that this relationship exists because employees who have been with the organization longer are typically ignored by the organization. Many of the firm's motivational efforts are focused on newer employees, while longer-term employees are assumed to be satisfied (Traut et al. 2000). Additionally, longer-term employees are often viewed as being a hindrance to organizational change (Griffith 1997). In some cases, employees have longer job tenure not because of their satisfaction with the position, but because of job security or the need to protect investments such as earned leave, insurance benefits, or retirement plans.

The match between an employee's expected and actual job conditions has long been recognized as a determinate of job satisfaction, with employee age and education viewed as key variables in the relationship (cf. Martin and Shehan 1989). Age has been shown to influence job satisfaction, with older employees exhibiting the highest levels. Greater job satisfaction among older employees is thought to occur because they expect less from their jobs than their younger counterparts, either because they are less educated or because their standards have eroded to the point where they demand less (Morris and Villemez 1992). Alternatively, it has been suggested that older employees exhibit higher job satisfaction because of higher levels of perceived control, experiential capital, and their increased ability to cope with stress (Hochwarter et al. 2001).

Support exists for a negative relationship between an employee's level of education and their job satisfaction. Blue-collar workers who failed to obtain a college degree reported lower levels of satisfaction than did blue-collar workers who never attended college (Quinn and Mandilovitch 1975). Similarly, a study of postal workers found education to be negatively related to satisfaction with supervisors and pay (Johnson and Johnson 2000). Highly educated employees may experience less satisfaction due to feelings of being overqualified for their positions (Johnson, Morrow, and Johnson 2002). Employees who perceive themselves as being overqualified tend to have higher expectations and a greater need for intrinsic rewards (Martin and Shehan 1989). Viewed collectively, previous research suggests that higher education levels lead to higher workplace expectations. This conclusion is troubling for the service industry, as most service positions offer little in the way of significant intrinsic rewards.

Individual Differences and Self-Efficacy

Self-efficacy–an employee's belief in his or her ability to perform job-related tasks–grows stronger over time as the employee successfully performs tasks and builds the confidence necessary to fulfill their role in the organization (Bandura 1977; Gist and Mitchell 1992). One of the primary determinants of self-efficacy is enactive mastery, which Bandura (1982) defines as past performance accomplishments in the relevant task. As an employee is given opportunities to perform a particular task and succeed, the employee's skills, confidence, and coping abilities become stronger. These situations are paramount in service firms, where the job demands that employees learn and adapt to unique customer requirements (Hartline and Ferrell 1996). As an employee spends more time in a service position, he or she has more opportunities to practice these skills, subsequently increasing their level of self-efficacy.

There is reason to believe that self-efficacy may decline with age due to organizational, social, psychological, and physiological processes that undermine enactive mastery and self-efficacy beliefs (Maurer 2001). Research suggests that fewer older employees participate in on-the-job training (Cleveland and Shore 1992), and that older employees tend to be outperformed in training by their younger counterparts (Kubeck et al. 1996). As a result, older employees have fewer opportunities for enactive mastery, thereby lowering self-efficacy. Physiological or health issues may also affect self-efficacy (Bandura 1977). Negative performance experiences by older employees may serve as a source of anxiety, and therefore elicit fear of failure during future work experiences (Maurer 2001).

Individual Differences and Role Stress

The stress created by spanning the boundary between the demands of the firm and the demands of customers is considered to be an unavoidable fact-of-life for service employees (Singh 2000). Unfortunately, past research sheds little light on the relationships among employee characteristics and the primary role stress dimensions of conflict and ambiguity. Early research on role conflict found evidence that experienced employees (salespeople) encountered less conflict than less experienced employees (Walker, Churchill, and Ford 1975). This is likely due to employees learning to cope with role demands as they gain experience in the industry. This same effect seems to hold true for job tenure, as employees who spend a greater amount of time in a job learn to handle the demands of the job more effectively (Fisher and Gitelson 1983).

The relationships between role stress and employee age and education are not well understood. Fisher and Gitelson (1983) found a weak, negative relationship between age and role stress, suggesting that older employees are better able to handle the demands of their jobs. However, other researchers have found no evidence of a link between age or education and role stress (cf. Howell, Bellenger, and Wilcox 1987; Liou 1995).

Individual Differences and Organizational Commitment

Organizational commitment is generally defined as an affective attachment to, identification with, and involvement in an organization (Allen and Meyer 1993). Some evidence exists that commitment declines as employees spend more time in a job, but increases with experience in an industry. This seems to occur due to differing expectations about the job vis-à-vis the industry. Meyer and Allen (1988) found that commitment declines significantly after the first year on the job because employees enter organizations with unrealistic expectations. As employees spend more time in an industry, however, their expectations become more realistic and their commitment grows stronger (Mowday, Porter, and Steers 1982).

Interestingly, however, Allen and Meyer (1993) found that industry experience and job tenure may be surrogates for employee age, which they argued is more important in determining employee commitment. Older employees exhibit stronger commitment because they have satisfied most of their needs for belongingness, security, and self-esteem. Older employees are also more mature and exhibit significantly stronger feelings of obligation to the organization than their younger counterparts (Allen and Meyer 1993; Cherrington, Condie, and England 1979). Taken together, these results suggest that while commitment appears to be associated with experience and job tenure, it is driven largely by age and not work experience. This conclusion is problematic for the service industry, where employees tend to be younger rather than older.

Previous research gives some indication that individual differences are associated with employee responses that are critical to service delivery. However, none of these studies have examined these individual differences and responses concurrently. Further, few of these studies occur within services or use service employees as the sampling frame. Our study is designed to overcome these shortcomings by determining which individual difference variables are most closely associated with employees' job satisfaction, self-efficacy, role stress, and organizational commitment.

RESEARCH METHODOLOGY

Sample

Hotels were selected as the sampling frame because the employee respondents are likely to exhibit significant variation in both individual differences and job-related responses. Hotels are also widely studied in the literature, thereby making our results comparable to previous studies. To obtain a sample, the marketing directors of several hotel chains were contacted. Each chain is similar with respect to quality and price, and are frequented by both business and leisure travelers. Three chains agreed to participate and provided mailing lists of their hotel managers.

Hotel managers were contacted by senior executives to explain the research and ask for their support. Approximately two weeks later, questionnaire packets–each containing five employee surveys and postage-paid return envelopes–were mailed to each hotel manager. Due to constraints imposed by the participating chains, we were not allowed to contact employees directly. Consequently, the hotel managers were instructed to distribute the employee surveys across a variety of service positions. Approximately two months after the initial mailing, a second wave of materials was mailed. All questionnaires were returned directly to the researchers.

Questionnaires were returned by 743 employees (33.5% response rate). A time-trend extrapolation test (Armstrong and Overton 1977) revealed no differences between early and late respondents on demographic characteristics or job-related responses. The characteristics of the respondents are typical of the industry as most are 20 to 30 years of age (63.8%), have some college education (43.3%), and work in front desk or customer service positions (53.7%).

Measures

To remain consistent with previous research, the job-related response variables were measured using existing scales (see Table 1). The individual difference variables were assessed in one of two ways. To measure industry experience and job tenure, respondents were asked to indicate their years of experience in the hotel industry and years in their present position with their firm. To measure age, respondents were asked to mark one of nine categories ranging from "Under 20" to "Over 60." Education was measured in a similar fashion using six categories that ranged from "Some high school" to "Hold a graduate degree."

Analysis

Based on the frequency distribution of the individual difference variables, a median split was used to classify respondents into high and low experience and job tenure groups. Given the categorical nature of the age and education variables, and their resulting frequency distributions, respondents were reclassified into high, moderate, and low age and education groups. A multiple analysis-of-variance (GLM) procedure was employed to test for mean differences across the job-related response variables. These results, shown in Table 2, indicate that significant differences exist across the experience, job tenure, age, and education groupings. However, there were no significant interactions among the

TABLE 1. Measures Used in the Study

Construct	Sources	Operationalization	Reliability[a]
Job Satisfaction	Brown & Peterson (1993)	A 5-item scale that measures the extent to which employees are satisfied with a variety of job dimensions.	.822
Self-Efficacy	Jones (1986)	An 8-item scale that measures the extent to which employees exhibit confidence in their job skills and abilities.	.672
Role Stress	Chonko, Howell, & Bellenger (1986)	The 12-item role conflict and 17-item role ambiguity scales were combined to measure the extent to which employees experience role stress in the performance of their jobs.	.923
Organizational Commitment	Mathieu & Zajac (1990); Mowday, Steers, & Porter (1979)	An 8-item scale that measures the affective (attitudinal) commitment of employees.[b]	.913

[a]Reliability estimates are Cronbach's alpha.
[b] Mathieu and Zajac (1990) found that the 15-item commitment scale of Mowday et al. (1979) contained two dimensions: affective commitment and desire to remain with the organization. The scale items used here are those from the affective commitment dimension.

individual difference variables. Based on these findings, the univariate results were examined to assess the effect of each individual difference variable on employees' job-related responses. These results are reported in Table 3.

RESULTS AND DISCUSSION

The tests for mean differences are reported in Tables 4 and 5. The results indicate that the high experience group exhibits significantly less role stress and greater commitment than does the low experience group. Industry experience has no effect on job satisfaction or self-efficacy. These results tend to support previous studies and suggest that more experienced employees are better able to handle the demands of their jobs. Further, experienced employees may exhibit greater commitment due to the more realistic expectations they hold about their jobs. The lack of a relationship between industry experience and job satisfaction and self-efficacy does not support previous research. However, our results are not surprising, given the nature of these constructs. Satisfaction and

TABLE 2. Multivariate Results: Effects of Individual Differences on Employee Attitudes and Responses

Source	df	Wilk's Lambda	F	p	η^2
Intercept	4	.016	9232.48	.000	.984
Industry Experience (IE)	4	.981	3.05	.017	.019
Job Tenure (JT)	4	.954	7.46	.000	.046
Age (A)	8	.971	2.25	.022	.014
Education (E)	8	.955	3.63	.000	.023
IE × JT	4	.990	1.51	.197	.010
IE × A	8	.987	1.05	.396	.007
IE × E	8	.989	0.82	.586	.005
JT × A	8	.980	1.53	.141	.010
JT × E	8	.985	1.20	.295	.008
A × E	16	.974	1.00	.449	.006
IE × JT × A	8	.995	0.38	.931	.002
IE × JT × E	8	.984	1.23	.278	.008
IE × A × E	16	.973	1.06	.386	.007
JT × A × E	16	.976	0.96	.499	.006
IE × JT × A × E	16	.985	0.57	.905	.004
Error	619				

TABLE 3. Univariate Results: Effects of Individual Differences on Employee Attitudes and Responses

Source	Job Satisfaction		Self-Efficacy		Role Stress		Organizational Commitment	
	F	p	F	p	F	p	F	p
Intercept	7467.98	.000	6739.19	.000	3780.77	.000	5419.33	.000
Industry Experience (IE)	0.26	.608	2.01	.157	6.97	.008	3.37	.067
Job Tenure (JT)	15.83	.000	17.55	.000	0.19	.660	18.02	.000
Age (A)	2.82	.060	0.17	.848	0.08	.922	7.02	.001
Education (E)	1.16	.314	8.64	.000	1.65	.192	3.40	.034
Corrected Model	2.03	.001	3.25	.000	1.62	.015	2.23	.000

Note: Due to the nonsignificance of all interaction terms, they have been omitted for clarity.

TABLE 4. Means Tests for Industry Experience and Job Tenure

	Industry Experience			Job Tenure		
	Low (345)	High (386)	Sig.	Low (389)	High (338)	Sig.
Job Satisfaction	3.623	3.666	.608	3.813	3.477	.000
Self-Efficacy	5.210	5.033	.157	4.860	5.383	.000
Role Stress	2.083	1.911	.008	2.011	1.983	.660
Organizational Commitment	5.034	5.292	.067	5.461	4.866	.000

Note: A Bonferroni adjustment was made for multiple comparisons. Sample sizes for each group are in parentheses.

self-efficacy are both *job-related*, whereas industry experience is relevant across a variety of jobs, even within the same industry.

Job tenure holds significant relationships with satisfaction, self-efficacy, and commitment. Employees in the low tenure group exhibit significantly more satisfaction and commitment, but hold weaker self-efficacy beliefs. While these results are somewhat supportive of previous studies, they present a considerable challenge for service managers. Newer employees with less time on the job are likely to be satisfied and committed to organization–both desirable outcomes. However, these employees tend to lack the feelings of self-efficacy that are so crucial to effective service delivery (cf. Hartline and Ferrell 1996). Over time, these relationships shift as satisfaction and commitment decline, while self-efficacy beliefs become stronger (Meyer and Allen 1988; Traut et al. 2000). This situation also represents a challenge for managers as they attempt to maintain satisfaction and commitment, and hence service

TABLE 5. Means Tests for Employee Age and Education

| | Employee Age | | | | Employee Education | | | |
	Low (327)	Mod (152)	High (250)	Sig.	Low (234)	Mod (311)	High (185)	Sig.
Job Satisfaction	3.579[a]	3.572	3.784[a]	.060	3.627	3.722	3.585	.314
Self-Efficacy	5.106	5.175	5.084	.848	4.766[ab]	5.137[ac]	5.462[bc]	.000
Role Stress	2.013	1.995	1.984	.922	1.970	1.945	2.076	.192
Organizational Commitment	5.100[a]	4.867[b]	5.523[ab]	.001	5.204	5.349[a]	4.936[a]	.034

Note: A Bonferroni adjustment was made for multiple comparisons. Significantly different means are denoted by common superscripts. Sample sizes for each group are in parentheses.

quality, over time. Finally, the lack of a relationship between job tenure and role stress was not expected. However, this finding provides further evidence that stress is inherent to the service industry and is not likely to change over time.

Employee age has a significant effect on job satisfaction and commitment, with older employees exhibiting higher scores on both variables. Many researchers argue that older employees expect less and are more mature than younger employees, thereby allowing them to be happier with their jobs and more committed to their organizations (Allen and Meyer 1993; Morris and Villemez 1992). While most service employees tend to be younger rather than older, many firms in the retail and fast food industries have had great success in hiring older employees. The fact that age has no relationship with self-efficacy and role stress supports previous work and serves to further underscore the intrinsic nature of service positions. Since the tasks associated with the job are not that complex, employees may hold uniformly high self-efficacy beliefs that are unlikely to change with age. Further, age may have little effect on role stress because younger and older employees alike suffer under the stress of the job.

Employees' educational level is associated with both self-efficacy and commitment, with highly educated employees exhibiting the strongest self-efficacy beliefs and moderately educated employees exhibiting higher commitment. The relationship between education and self-efficacy is logical, though it has not been demonstrated previously in the literature. We note that the employees in our sample exhibit moderate to high levels of self-efficacy regardless of their educational attainment, likely an inherent aspect of the routine tasks associated with their positions. Likewise, the relationship between education and commitment, though somewhat weak in our study, has not been demonstrated previously. The lack of a relationship between education and role stress is not surprising given the results of previous studies (cf. Howell et al. 1987; Liou 1995). On the other hand, the fact that education does not affect job satisfaction is surprising and is contrary to previous research. We note, however, that previous work on the education/ satisfaction relationship does not occur in the same context as our study. It may be that the nature of service positions, with their relatively low levels of intrinsic rewards, is such that job satisfaction stays relatively uniform across employee education levels.

IMPLICATIONS AND DIRECTIONS FOR FUTURE RESEARCH

Before discussing the implications of our study, we note its limitations. First, our study's focus on a single industry may raise concerns about generalizability. However, this approach eliminates problems associated with the effects of differences across industries. Further, the constructs examined in our study could be applied to essentially any industry, thereby increasing the generalizability of our results. Second, because we could not contact employees directly, we had to rely on hotel managers to distribute the surveys. While we recognize the potential for bias associated with this procedure, we do not believe it had any appreciable impact on response quality. The managers did not know the purpose of the study beforehand, therefore they had no reason to distribute the surveys in a biased fashion. Finally, though we focused on constructs that have a demonstrated connection to service quality, our study could have included any number of potentially viable constructs from the human resources or marketing literatures. For example, in their early work on service employee management, Parasuraman, Berry, and Zeithaml (1990) argued that constructs such as employee-job fit, horizontal communication, and task standardization could affect service employees and their delivery of quality service. Our study could be extended in future research by examining how individual characteristics affect employees' shared values, organizational citizenship behaviors, or adaptability/innovation during the service encounter.

Managerial Implications

Our study indicates that easily identifiable employee characteristics are associated with the employee attitudes and responses that are necessary for the effective delivery of quality service. Our results offer some interesting insights into the recruitment, selection, and retention of service employees. They also point to some challenges that service firms and their managers must overcome in an effort to balance internal and external relationship management.

Managers must make some essential tradeoffs in recruiting and selecting employees for service positions. Across many services, the typical employee is a high school or college-age student who has held several jobs, many of them being part-time. As a result, these potential employees have relatively little experience in any one industry, relatively short tenure in any one job, and less education (though it is likely to be ongoing). Based on our results, potential employees possessing these characteristics are likely to be less committed, less satisfied, have lower self-efficacy, and suffer from role stress. Some of these negative effects are offset by their shorter job tenure and relatively lower education. Overall, our results suggest that the "typical" service employee is likely to be incapable of exhibiting the necessary attitudes and responses that are conducive to superior service quality.

Given that, how should managers proceed in recruiting employees to fill service positions? Our findings indicate that the "best" service employee may be an older person who possesses a great deal of industry experience. These individuals are likely to be more satisfied with their jobs, more committed to the firm, and better able to handle the stress associated with the service position. They are also likely to be better educated. Given the fact that most service positions offer little in the way of intrinsic rewards or high levels of pay, this combination of employee characteristics and responses could be quite important in maintaining employee morale, reducing absenteeism or turnover, and increasing employee retention. The hiring of older employees in service positions has been rising in recent years due to the shrinking number of younger, more typical employees in the labor pool (Prince 2002). On the whole, firms that hire older employees have been impressed by their work ethic and loyalty.

Unfortunately, hiring older, more experienced employees presents some challenges. Many of these individuals do not need to work or may already be working for a competitor. Therefore, they might not be interested in accepting a new position. Stealing employees from competitors is a growing option, but is ultimately self-defeating in that the firm itself is vulnerable from attacks by competitors (Spaulding 1999). Hiring older, more experienced employees is also more expensive than hiring typical service employees. Managers may have to pay higher wages to get these employees. In addition, hiring older employees increases the costs associated with health benefits and workdays lost due to illness

(Prince 2002). In the future, service firms may have little choice but to absorb these costs and hire older, experienced employees as the pool of younger employees continues to shrink. Service firms have yet to truly face this conundrum of balancing the need for effective, responsive employees and the costs associated with acquiring and retaining them.

Future Research

Our findings suggest several directions for future research. First, our study could be replicated within other services (i.e., branch banking, retail stores, restaurants) or in professional services (i.e., insurance, health care, financial services) to further examine how individual differences affect employee attitudes and responses. In professional services, where employees see their jobs as career choices, these relationships are likely to differ.

Second, future research could investigate whether organizational commitment is based more on employees' perceived career opportunities rather than educational attainment. Our findings indicate that moderately educated employees (associated with "some college" on the questionnaire) exhibit the highest commitment, thereby revealing an inverted U-shaped relationship between education and commitment. Are employees in the low education group (associated with "some high school" and "high school graduate") less committed because they see their jobs as being "dead end" with little opportunity for advancement? Likewise, are highly educated employees (associated with "college graduate" and "graduate degree") less committed because they aspire to higher-level career goals than is afforded them in their current position? In these situations, moderately educated employees may exhibit higher commitment because they *expect* to move beyond their current position. In other words, these employees might be committed *for the time being* because the job and the organization fulfill their current needs and expectations.

Finally, future research could investigate whether individual characteristics can act as surrogates for employees' perceived overqualification. In particular, younger, more educated, or experienced employees may exhibit less conducive attitudes and responses due to higher expectations and the need for greater intrinsic rewards (Johnson et al. 2002; Martin and Shehan 1989). Given that many service positions fail to meet these requirements, overqualification could be an important issue for researchers and managers to address.

REFERENCES

Al-Ajmi, R. (2001). The Effect of Personal Characteristics on Job Satisfaction: A Study Among Male Managers in the Kuwait Oil Industry. *International Journal of Contemporary Management, 11* (3/4), 91-110.

Allen, N.J. and Meyer, J.P. (1993). Organizational Commitment: Evidence of Career Stage Effects? *Journal of Business Research,* (26), 49-61.

Anthony, W.P., Perrewe, P.L., and Kacmar, K.M. (1993). *Strategic Human Resource Management,* Harcourt Brace Jovanovich, Orlando, FL.

Armstrong, J.S. and Overton, T.S. (1977). Estimating Nonresponse Bias in Mail Surveys. *Journal of Marketing Research, 14* (August), 396-402.

Bandura, A. (1977). *Social Learning Theory,* Englewood Cliffs, NJ: Prentice-Hall.

Bandura, A. (1982). Self-Efficacy Mechanism in Human Agency. *American Psychologist,* (37), 122-147.

Behling, O. (1998). Employee Selection: Will Intelligence and Conscientiousness Do the Job? *Academy of Management Executive, 12* (1), 77-86.

Berry, L.L. and Parasuraman, A. (1992). Services Marketing Starts from Within. *Marketing Management,* (Winter), 25-34.

Bilgic, R. (1998). The Relationship Between Job Satisfaction and Personal Characteristics of Turkish Workers. *The Journal of Psychology,* (32), 549-561.

Brown, S.P. and Peterson, R.A. (1993). Antecedents and Consequences of Salesperson Job Satisfaction: Meta-Analysis and Assessment of Causal Effects. *Journal of Marketing Research, 30* (February), 63-77.

Cherrington, D.J., Condie, S.J., and England, J.L. (1979). Age and Work Values. *Academy of Management Journal,* (22), 617-623.

Chonko, L.B., Howell, R.D., and Bellenger, D.N. (1986). Congruence in Sales Force Evaluations: Relation to Sales Force Perceptions of Conflict and Ambiguity. *Journal of Personal Selling and Sales Management, 6* (May), 35-48.

Cleveland, J. and Shore, L. (1992). Self- and Supervisory Perspectives on Age and Work Attitudes and Performance. *Journal of Applied Psychology,* (77), 469-484.

Decker, P. and Borgen, F. (1993). Dimensions of Work Appraisal: Stress, Strain, Coping, Job Satisfaction, and Negative Affectivity. *Journal of Counseling Psychology, 40* (October), 470-478.

Fisher, C.D. and Gitelson, R. (1983). A Meta-Analysis of the Correlates of Role Conflict and Ambiguity. *Journal of Applied Psychology, 68,* 320-333.

Gist, M.E. and Mitchell, T.R. (1992). Self-Efficacy: A Theoretical Analysis of Its Determinants and Malleability. *Academy of Management Review, 17* (April), 183-211.

Griffith, V. (1997). Still Keeping Up as Time Goes By. *Financial Times,* (June 2), 16-19.

Hartline, M.D. and Ferrell, O.C. (1996). The Management of Customer-Contact Service Employees: An Empirical Investigation. *Journal of Marketing, 60* (October), 52-70.

Hochwarter, W.A., Ferris, G.R., Perrewe, P.L., Witt, L.A., and Kiewitz C. (2001). A Note on the Nonlinearity of the Age-Job Satisfaction Relationship. *Journal of Applied Social Psychology, 31* (6), 1223-1237.

Howell, R.D., Bellenger, D.N., and Wilcox, J.B. (1987). Self-Esteem, Role Stress, and Job Satisfaction Among Marketing Managers. *Journal of Business Research, 15* (February), 71-85.

Johnson, G.J. and Johnson, W.R. (2000). Perceived Overqualification and Dimensions of Job Satisfaction: A Longitudinal Analysis. *The Journal of Psychology, 134* (5), 537-555.

Johnson, R.W., Morrow, P.C., and Johnson, G.J. (2002). An Evaluation of a Perceived Overqualification Scale Across Work Settings. *The Journal of Psychology, 136* (4), 425-441.

Jones, G.R. (1986). Socialization Tactics, Self-Efficacy, and Newcomers' Adjustments to Organizations. *Academy of Management Journal, 29* (June), 262-79.

Kubeck, J., Delp, N., Haslett, T., and McDaniel, M. (1996). Does Job-Related Training Performance Decline with Age? *Psychology and Aging,* (11), 92-107.

Liou, K.T. (1995). Role Stress and Job Stress Among Detention Care Workers. *Criminal Justice and Behavior, 22* (December), 425-36.

Martin, J.K. and Shehan, C.L. (1989). Education and Job Satisfaction: The Influences of Gender, Wage-Earning Status, and Job Values. *Work and Occupations, 16* (2), 184-199.

Mathieu, J.E. and Zajac, D.M. (1990). A Review and Meta-Analysis of the Antecedents, Correlates, and Consequences of Organizational Commitment. *Psychological Bulletin, 108* (September), 171-94.

Maurer, T.J. (2001). Career-Relevant Learning and Development, Worker Age, and Beliefs About Self-Efficacy for Development. *Journal of Management, 27* (2), 123-40.

Meyer, J.P. and Allen, N.J. (1988). Links Between Work Experiences and Organizational Commitment During the First Year of Employment. *Journal of Occupational Psychology, 61,* 195-209.

Morris, J.M. and Villemez, W.J. (1992). Mobility Potential and Job Satisfaction: Mixing Dispositional and Situational Explanations. *Work and Occupations, 19* (1), 35-58.

Mowday, R.T., Porter, L.M., and Steers, R.M. (1982). *Employee-Organization Linkages: The Psychology of Commitment, Absenteeism, and Turnover,* Academic Press, New York.

Mowday, R.T., Steers, R.M., and Porter, L.M. (1979). The Measurement of Organizational Commitment. *Journal of Vocational Behavior, 14* (April), 224-47.

O'Hara, B.S., Boles, J.S., and Johnston, M.W. (1991). The Influence of Personal Variables on Salesperson Selling Orientation. *Journal of Personal Selling and Sales Management, 11* (1), 61-67.

Parasuraman, A., Berry, L.L., Zeithaml, V.A. (1990). An Empirical Examination of Relationships in an Extended Service Quality Model. *Marketing Science Institute Working Paper Series,* Report No. 90-122. Cambridge, MA: Marketing Science Institute.

Prince, M. (2002). Graying of America Challenges Employers. *Business Insurance, 36* (August), 1, 16.

Quinn, R.P. and Mandilovitch, M.S.B. (1975). *Education and Job Satisfaction: A Questionable Payoff,* Ann Arbor: Institute for Survey Research.

Schneider, B. and Bowen, D.E. (1985). Employee and Customer Perceptions of Service in Banks. *Journal of Applied Psychology, 70* (3), 423-433.

Singh, J. (2000). Performance Productivity and Quality of Frontline Employees in Service Organizations. *Journal of Marketing, 64* (April), 15-34.

Spaulding, M.A. (1999). Retaining Good Workers Is a Full-Time Job. *Converting Magazine*, 17 (July), 6.

Taber, T. and Alliger, G. (1995). A Task-Level Assessment of Job Satisfaction. *Journal of Organizational Behavior*, (16), 101-121.

Traut, C.A., Larsen, R., and Feimer, S.H. (2000). Hanging On or Fading Out? Job Satisfaction and the Long-Term Worker. *Public Personnel Management, 29* (3), 343-51.

Walker, O.C., Churchill, G.A., and Ford, N.M. (1975). Organizational Determinants of the Industrial Salesmen's Role Conflict and Ambiguity. *Journal of Marketing, 39* (January), 32-39.

Boundary Spanners' Satisfaction with Organizational Support Services: An Internal Communications Perspective

Simona Stan

University of Oregon

Timothy D. Landry

University of Oklahoma

Kenneth R. Evans

University of Missouri-Columbia

Simona Stan, PhD, is Assistant Professor of Marketing, University of Oregon, 1208 University of Oregon, Eugene, OR 97403 (E-mail: sstan@lcbmail. uoregon.edu). Her research interests include services marketing, relationship marketing, and organizational support to salespeople. Dr. Stan's work appears in the *Journal of EuroMarketing*, *Journal of East-West Business*, *International Marketing Review*, and others.

Timothy D. Landry, PhD, is Assistant Professor of Marketing and Supply Chain Management, Michael F. Price COB, University of Oklahoma, 307 West Brooks, 1L Norman, OK 73019 (E-mail: tlandry@ou.edu). His research interests include sales and retail management. Dr. Landry's research has appeared in the *Journal of the Academy of Marketing Science*, the *Journal of Personal Selling and Sales Management*, and others.

Kenneth R. Evans, PhD, is Professor of Marketing and Associate Dean of Graduate Studies, College of Business, University of Missouri-Columbia, Cornell Hall, Columbia, MO 65201 (E-mail: evansk@missouri.edu). His research interests include marketing management, sales/sales management, marketing theory, and services marketing. Dr. Evans' research has appeared in the *Journal of Marketing*, *Journal of the Academy of Marketing Science*, *Journal of Personal Selling and Sales Management*, *Industrial Marketing Management*, *Journal of Advertising*, and others. Dr. Evans serves on the editorial review boards of a number of the disciplines' top journals.

[Haworth co-indexing entry note]: "Boundary Spanners' Satisfaction with Organizational Support Services: An Internal Communications Perspective." Stan, Simona, Timothy D. Landry, and Kenneth R. Evans. Co-published simultaneously in *Journal of Relationship Marketing* (Best Business Books, an imprint of The Haworth Press, Inc.) Vol. 3, No. 2/3, 2004, pp. 43-63; and: *Internal Relationship Management: Linking Human Resources to Marketing Performance* (ed: Michael D. Hartline, and David Bejou) Best Business Books, an imprint of The Haworth Press, Inc., 2004, pp. 43-63. Single or multiple copies of this article are available for a fee from The Haworth Document Delivery Service [1-800-HAWORTH, 9:00 a.m. - 5:00 p.m. (EST). E-mail address: docdelivery@haworthpress.com].

http://www.haworthpress.com/web/JRM
© 2004 by The Haworth Press, Inc. All rights reserved.
Digital Object Identifier: 10.1300/J366v03n02_04

43

SUMMARY. Internal services (i.e., support services) are an important form of organizational support for external boundary spanners (e.g., salespeople, customer service representatives). Internal services such as information systems, market research, training, accounting, and facilities support are intended to allow boundary spanners to better serve the firm's customer. Little research, however, has addressed factors that influence a boundary spanner's satisfaction with such services. The research presented here offers insight into how internal communication by both managers and service providers impacts a boundary spanner's satisfaction with support services. Results indicate that service provider and manager communications are largely complementary and that satisfaction with service outcomes, rather than service quality, appears to have an enduring impact upon a boundary spanner's overall job satisfaction. Implications for future research are addressed. *[Article copies available for a fee from The Haworth Document Delivery Service: 1-800-HAWORTH. E-mail address: <docdelivery@haworthpress.com> Website: <http://www.HaworthPress. com> © 2004 by The Haworth Press, Inc. All rights reserved.]*

KEYWORDS. Organizational support services, internal services, boundary spanner, internal communications, internal marketing, sales management, socialization

Customer contact employees, such as salespeople and customer service reps, are boundary spanning employees engaged in exchanges with external constituencies. These boundary spanners largely determine the effectiveness of a marketing effort since they are responsible for the delivery of value to customers and the generation of organizational revenues. As competitive pressures continue to rise, organizations challenge these boundary spanners to enhance customer satisfaction and further customer relationships in order to increase profitability (Crosby, Evans and Cowles 1990). Such pressures call for these employees to access the necessary tools and resources to identify and meet a broad range of customer needs. This, in turn, places demands back on the organization to properly support the boundary spanner (Bitner 1995; Evans, Arnold and Grant 1999; Schneider and Bowen 1995). There is growing evidence for strong correlations among the quality of organizational support, the boundary spanner's performance, and customer satisfaction (Davis 1991; Rust et al. 1996; Schneider, White and Paul 1998). Thus, an organization's ability to provide effective, high quality support to its boundary spanning employees may be an important source of competitive advantage (Heskett et al. 1994).

A critical form of organizational support is internal services provision, such as information systems, market research, training, accounting, and facilities supports, which provides boundary spanners with the needed resources to serve and satisfy customers (Berry and Parasuraman 1991; Davis 1991). While boundary spanners are not charged directly for these services, internal support services are hoped to be valuable and thus utilized by the boundary spanning employee. Organizations face significant challenges, however, in the design and delivery of support services. On the one hand, boundary spanners desire high quality support services in terms of flexibility, availability, and responsiveness to their specific requests (Gremler, Bitner and Evans 1994). Boundary spanners who are not satisfied with organization's support services may be motivated to find alternative ways of sourcing those services. They may perform part of those services by themselves, use informal personal connections within the firm to circumvent the system to obtain more or faster service, or use service providers other than those sanctioned by the organization. Such practices are dysfunctional for both the organization and the boundary spanner (Finn et al. 1996; Lovelock 1991). On the other hand, providing highly flexible, timely and customized support services can be costly (Davis 1991; Hays 1996), and in the present era of efficiency, organizations are under continuous pressure to reduce the costs of internal operations (Mills and Ungson 2001). The total quality management paradigm of the previous decades, centered on satisfying or delighting internal customers with excellent internal service delivery (cf. Rafiq and Ahmed 1995), is thus often tempered by a focus on the efficient delivery and utilization of support services by their intended users (Burrows 2001).

A key challenge to this approach is imparting to users an understanding of the organization's support limitations and the organization's procedures regarding the support service interface. It is fundamental to socialize employees to the organization's support services in order to create realistic expectations of those services. Yet, managers and service providers, though generally aware of the need to provide high quality support services, often fail to effectively communicate an understanding of the internal support services' purposes and resources (Stauss 1995).

Unfortunately, the extant research on internal service quality has neglected to investigate the impact of organizational communication on developing internal customers' perceptions of the organization's support services. While research in consumer services marketing acknowledges the importance of socializing consumers to the service organization (e.g., Mills and Morris 1986), there is little understanding of how internal communication helps employees in general, and boundary spanners in particular, to develop a better understanding of, and a more positive attitude toward, an organization's support services. The research presented here addresses this gap by exploring ways in which communication from organizational service providers and managers impacts boundary spanner's perceptions of support services and related service outcomes.

BACKGROUND

The boundary spanner interface with support services is different from that of the employee working within the boundary of the organization. Internal clients of support services have been described as a captive market–they are likely to be passive consumers of support services who do not pursue alternative sources for support services even when dissatisfied, and they tend to accept internal support service conditions with resignation (Nagel and Cilliers 1990). Boundary spanners, however, are involved in exchanges with external constituencies who have little understanding of the support services that boundary spanners receive. Customers simply expect a quality service delivery. As such, high performing boundary spanners are likely to buffer the gaps in weak organizational support services in order to maintain customer relationships. As a result, boundary spanners have been found to experience high stress, low job satisfaction, and high turnover when forced to deal with support inadequacies (Wetzler, de Ruyter and Lemmink 1999).

In consuming the support service, boundary spanners engage in an exchange of information with both the service provider and the management of the organization (cf. Mills and Ungson 2001). To promote support services utilization, both groups need to be effective in informing boundary spanners about the nature and capabilities of the support service (Stauss 1995). Since it is often the organization's management who specifies the support service design and sets service delivery policies (Mills and Ungson 2001), management is in the position to impact boundary spanner satisfaction with support services by communicating appropriate expectations about service delivery and the benefits of the service (i.e., service outcomes). The internal service provider also plays an important role in maintaining boundary spanner satisfaction through the management of boundary spanner expectations during service delivery and through satisfying boundary spanners' specific requests. Thus, successful internal support services depend largely on marketing the services to boundary spanners, by persuading them with the benefits of the service (a selling task) and by responding to specific questions, concerns, or needs of the boundary spanner (a relational task). In effect, boundary spanning employees should be viewed as support service customers, and communication between (1) the service provider and the boundary spanner and (2) management and the boundary spanner about the internal support service should play an important role in boundary spanners' satisfaction with support services (see Figure 1).

CONCEPTUAL FRAMEWORK

Boundary Spanner Satisfaction with Support Services

The limited body of literature on internal services, being founded in the total quality management paradigm, stresses perceptions of *internal service quality*, or the quality of the service delivery, as an indicator of successful internal service provision (e.g., Brooks, Lings and Botschen 1999; Edvardsson and Gustavsson 1991; Finn et al. 1996). Studies per-

FIGURE 1. Conceptual Model

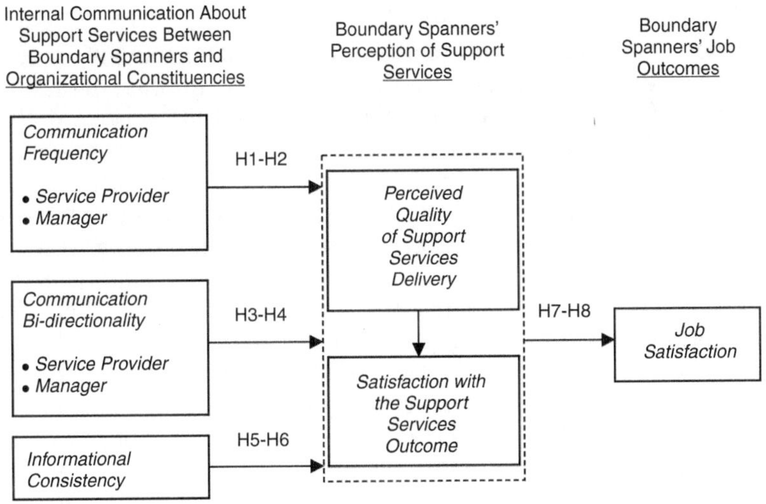

formed about various support services (e.g., purchasing, technical support) within a number of organizational contexts (e.g., hospitals, insurance firms) identify internal service quality as a key driver of employees' satisfaction with support services. However, it is argued here that in order to understand boundary spanners' satisfaction with support services, it is necessary to differentiate between perceived service delivery quality and satisfaction with the service outcome.

Though perceived service quality is an appropriate evaluation of service delivery for support service contexts, its typical focus on the "consumer" of the service (i.e., the employee) may leave untapped another key outcome for boundary spanners: satisfaction with how well the internal service support system helped boundary spanners to achieve their objectives. Conceptually, the closest parallel may be Holbrook's (1994) typology of customer value derived from service experiences, where it is argued that consumers derive value not only from the perceived quality of the service provision but also from *satisfaction with service outcomes*. Here, satisfaction derives, at least in part, from the support service's enhancement of the boundary spanner's capacity to serve and satisfy the external customer. Without explicitly tapping this aspect of satisfaction, researchers may be misrepresenting the totality of boundary spanners' "satisfaction" with support services.

In fact, the services marketing literature often makes the distinction between service outcomes and delivery evaluations, but does so as dimensions of the overall service quality concept. For example, Gronroos (1985) differentiates technical service quality (what is provided) from functional quality (how it is provided) and Rust and Oliver (1994) and Brady and Cronin (2001) differentiate service outcome quality from interaction quality. It is argued here, however, that in the case of organizational support services, the service outcome and the service delivery may be two different concepts, not two dimensions of the same concept. In internal services each is likely to be determined by different entities–with support service delivery being primarily specified by the service provider, and the support service outcome being primarily specified by the organization's management. Hence, support service providers may generate outstanding performance within their given specifications and constraints, yet boundary spanners may still end up dissatisfied with the service–again not because of a poor delivery process, but because they view the resulting benefits as inadequate. Thus, one contribution of this study is to suggest the usefulness of an extended conceptualization of successful internal support services–including perceptions of how the support service impacts other value-chain constituencies–in this case by including evaluations of how the internal service ultimately affects the boundary spanner's capacity to serve the external customer.

Communication Elements

Again, as boundary spanners constitute an internal market within the firm, the effective marketing of internal support services is important, and organizational communication may play a crucial role (Gummesson 1987). Research on organizational communication indicates that communication has two important aspects: structure and content. A third aspect, the mode of communication (i.e., formal versus informal) is often found to not significantly relate to service employee outcomes and was thus not included in this study (cf. Johlke and Duhan 2000). Communication structure represents the format or mannerisms by which communicators interact (Williams and Spiro 1985). In terms of structure, it has been suggested that more frequent and more bi-directional communication leads to more positive outcomes, such as relationship satisfaction and problem-solving between the communicating parties (e.g., Fisher, Maltz and Jaworski 1997; Johlke and Duhan 2000; Mohr and Nevin 1990; Mohr and Sohi 1995; Mohr, Fisher and Nevin 1996; Ruekert and Walker 1987).

Communication Frequency. From an internal marketing perspective, *communication frequency* should impact satisfaction with the service in at least two ways. First the communication frequency of the support service provider and, especially, of the boundary spanner's manager might initially indicate socializing, or selling, the boundary spanner on the importance of accepting internal service support. A stream of research in the services literature underscores the importance of consumer socialization to services (e.g., Hartline, Maxham and McKee 2000; Kelley, Donnelly and Skinner 1990; Mills and Morris 1986; Solomon et al. 1985). It could be argued that, similar to consumer socialization, internal customers need to be socialized in order to understand the value of support services and their relation to those services (Kelley, Donnelly and Skinner 1990; Mills and Morris 1986). Effectively socialized "customers" are more likely to develop realistic service expectations, engage in helpful behaviors, and be more satisfied with the service (Kelley, Skinner and Donnelly 1992). Additionally, substantial literature on organizational socialization of employees supports the idea that boundary spanners' satisfaction with support services is a function of socialization (e.g., Dubinsky et al. 1986; Evans et al. 1995; Johlke and Duhan 2000).

Second, communication frequency about the support service from managers, and especially the service support providers, should improve satisfaction through reducing uncertainty about what the support service can offer the boundary spanner and what functions the boundary spanner should perform to effectively utilize the support service. Boundary spanners may not have a clear understanding of the type, scope and actual performance of the internal service system (Stauss 1995). Researchers have found that uncertainty reduction has a positive impact on job satisfaction, organizational commitment and performance in sales and service contexts (e.g., Behrman, Bigoness and Perreault 1981; Dubinsky et al. 1986; Evans et al. 1995; Kelley, Donnelly and Skinner 1990; Mills and Morris 1986).

In sum, the process by which employees learn about what the organization considers as acceptable behaviors and attitudes is essentially communicative in nature. Employees develop initial interpretation schemes for their work environment, primarily through the communication received from others (cf. Jablin 1982). Thus, for boundary spanners, as communication frequency should relate to more accurate expectations about what the support service can provide, to an increased understanding of the boundary spanner's role in support service provision, and to an increased likelihood of being socialized to the value of support services, the following relationships are proposed:

H_1: Increased *communication frequency* by (a) boundary spanner management and (b) the internal support service provider will lead to higher perceptions of the *quality of the support service.*

H_2: Increased *communication frequency* by (a) boundary spanner management and (b) the internal support service provider will lead to greater *satisfaction with support service outcomes.*

Communication Bi-Directionality. Previous studies on interfunctional communication and customer relationship-building have posited that bi-directional communication relates to increased understanding between parties, commitment to relationships, and satisfaction (e.g., Mohr, Fisher and Nevin 1996; Jacobs et al. 2001). Communication bi-directionality increases the clarity and accuracy of the received message and therefore, increases the perceived quality of communication (e.g., Mohr and Sohi 1995). Moreover, communication bi-directionality may be indicative of collaborative problem solving or, at least, feedback regarding questions about the boundary spanner's role in support service consumption (cf. Jacobs et al. 2001). In a sense, active feedback from the organization may be a sign of an internal customer orientation toward the boundary spanner. As bi-directional communication serves to involve the boundary spanner in the support service and may be indicative of collaborative problem solving, the following hypotheses are posited:

> H_3: Increased *communication bi-directionality* by (a) boundary spanner management and (b) the internal support service provider will lead to higher perceptions of the *quality of the support service*.

> H_4: Increased *communication bi-directionality* by (a) boundary spanner management and (b) the internal support service provider will lead to greater *satisfaction with support service outcomes*.

Informational Consistency. In the case where there are multiple sources of communication (e.g., boundary spanner management, the internal support service provider), conflicting messages may create confusion for the receiver (Jablin 1987). For example, the communication of inconsistent or conflicting expectations about the boundary spanner's role in adopting or utilizing the service may induce role conflict, which is often posited as reducing role-related satisfaction (e.g., Biddle 1979; Katz and Kahn 1966). From a communications perspective, *informational consistency* is therefore likely to be an important concept in the study of the content of the communication flow. Some research, taking a more holistic approach toward the assessment of communication, suggests that summary evaluations of communication content such as informational consistency are important in predicting satisfaction with information exchanges (e.g., Mohr and Sohi 1995; Stohl and Redding 1987). As informational consistency may be an important predictor of boundary spanner satisfaction with the support service, the following hypotheses are offered:

> H_5: *Informational consistency* between boundary spanner management and the internal support service provider will lead to higher perceptions of the *quality of the support service*.

> H_6: *Informational consistency* between boundary spanner management and the internal support service provider will lead to higher perceptions of the *satisfaction with the service outcomes*.

The Effects of Satisfaction with Support Services

This study is the first to consider the broader impact of the satisfaction derived from the support service by exploring how it affects salespeople's overall job satisfaction. Job satisfaction is conceptualized as a global summary attitude reflecting an employee's contentment with his or her job (Teas 1983). Understanding the extent to which support services impact job satisfaction is important since job satisfaction is linked with a number of critical variables like stress, intention to quit, turnover, and performance (cf. Sergeant and Frenkel 2000). It is argued that employee satisfaction with the firm is influenced by service encounters with internal service providers (Berry and Parasuraman 1991; Gronroos 1985; George 1990). To the extent that ill-managed internal support services lead to service gaps with customers, decreased job satisfaction is likely (Bitner 1995; Heskett et al. 1994). Given the importance of the organization's support service system in the customer value-chain, boundary spanners' satisfaction with internal support services should impact their overall job satisfaction. By exploring overall job satisfaction's relationship with service quality and outcome satisfaction, the importance each aspect of service satisfaction should be made apparent. Thus, the following hypotheses are offered:

H_7: The *service quality* component of satisfaction with the internal support service will be positively related to *overall job satisfaction*.

H_8: The *outcome satisfaction* component of satisfaction with the internal support service will be positively related to *overall job satisfaction*.

METHODOLOGY

The empirical study was based upon a mailed survey administered to the sales force of a large financial investments firm, which provides a wide portfolio of financial products and investment services to consumers. The firm has more than 6,000 salespeople working in independent offices located in residential areas throughout the U.S. The firm is considered one of the best in the industry in terms of the quality of support services provided to its salespeople. A critical support service provided to salespeople starting their career with the firm is the provision of a sales office. The firm's facility services are responsible for finding the new office location, building or remodeling, furnishing the office, and negotiating the lease. Extensive interviews with the firm's management, support service providers, and salespeople indicated that the new office opening process, which lasts several months, is a critical event in a salesperson's career. The context provided by this firm is particularly suitable for the research objectives of this study because: (1) it offers a large sample of relatively independent boundary spanners who interact with many different sales managers; (2) the organization provides to these salespeople a centralized support service which is fairly standardized in terms of scope (i.e., a specified service outcome) and delivery policy; (3) there is a large variance in the extent to which salespeople communicate about the support service with managers and service providers; (4) other potential organizational and industry specific influences are controlled due to the use of a single firm.

The sample consists of a census of the 1,278 salespeople employed by the firm for whom a new office has been opened within two years of the data collection. In response to the initial and follow-up mailing, 830 usable questionnaires were returned for a 65% effective response rate. The salespeople in the sample were 83% male, mostly 26-55 years old (90%), possessed an average of 7.3 years of sales experience, and had worked for the firm an average of 18 months. Fifty-six percent of the salespeople were rated above the standard by their managers. The final sample characteristics closely match the characteristics of the firm's sales force, providing no evidence for non-response bias.

All construct measures consist of multi-item scales adapted from the existing literature or developed to fit the specific context of the study. With the exception of communication frequency and bi-directionality, which are measured with formative scales, all measures are unidimensional and have adequate Cronbach reliability coefficients. The measures, summarized in Table 1, consist of 7-point scales.

Perceived Quality of Support Service Delivery measures respondents' perceptions of the service provider's interactional performance: reliability, responsiveness, assurance, and empathy. The items are derived from the SERVQUAL scale by Parasuraman, Zeithaml and Berry (1985; 1988) and were adapted, based on interviews, to the specific situation investigated. The scale format is similar to SERVPERF (i.e., it asks respondents to report only performance perception and not expectations; cf. Cronin and Taylor 1992). Such an approach has been recommended and used in other studies of internal service quality (e.g., Finn et al. 1996; Rafiq and Ahmed 2000). As discussed, the service outcome

TABLE 1. Measures Used in the Study

Construct	Number of Items	Sample Item	Mean (St. Dev.)	Cronbach Reliability
Perceived Quality of Support Service Delivery	9	"the service providers were dependable"	4.6 (1.4)	0.93
Satisfaction with Support Service Outcome	6	"the office location meets your clients' needs"	5.7 (1.1)	0.90
Job Satisfaction	6	"I would advise a friend to work for this firm"	6.2 (0.95)	0.89
Communication Frequency with Service Provider	4	"face-to-face interaction"	1.7 (0.9)	Formative
Communication Frequency with Managers	3	"written documentation"	3.1 (2.6)	Formative
Communication Bi-directionality with Service Provider	3	"feedback about the office"	1.6 (1.1)	Formative
Communication Bi-directionality with Manager	3	"feedback about the office opening process"	2.7 (4.3)	Formative
Informational Consistency	2	"the received information has been consistent"	4.7 (1.5)	0.85

(i.e., the tangible output) has been separated from the service delivery process, which is consistent with recent service quality conceptualizations and operationalizations (cf. Brady and Cronin 2001). *Salespeople's Satisfaction with the Support Service Outcome* (i.e., the office in this research context), measures the extent to which the salespeople are satisfied with how the service meets their needs and their customers' needs. *Overall Job Satisfaction* is measured with a scale developed by Brown and Peterson (1994) for the context of direct selling. The *Communication Frequency* scales are formative measures of the respondents' estimated frequency with which they communicate with the sales managers and service providers by different modes (i.e., face-to-face, written, and phone or email) during the office opening process. The *Communication Bi-directionality* scales are formative measures of the extent to which the salespeople have provided and received feedback from the sales managers/service providers about office-related concerns. These scales are adapted from Mohr, Fisher and Nevin (1996). The *Informational Consistency* measure is based on Jablin (1982).

The proposed hypotheses were tested with path analysis, using LISREL 8.1. In specifying this model, each construct was represented by a single scale average score. This was done because four out of the eight measures are formative and the other measures are unidimensional. The missing data was deleted listwise. Very few cases (16) had missing data.

The final database for the path analysis consisted of 814 cases. All measures had adequately normal distributions and uncorrelated residuals, indicating that the basic assumptions for path analysis were met. In the first step, the hypothesized model was fit to the data; the path coefficients for each proposed relationship were thus estimated. Next, the model was revised by removing insignificant relationships. Finally, the model's overidentifying restrictions were relaxed, one at a time, to test for partial mediation effects of communication on job satisfaction. The Goodness-of-fit indices are reported in Table 2.

RESULTS

Table 2 and Figure 2 summarize the results of the path analysis used to test the proposed hypotheses. The hypothesized model has a fairly good fit to the data, but the chi-square is statistically significant ($p < 0.01$), indicating that there are overidentifying restrictions that should

TABLE 2. Path Analysis Results

	Hypothesized Model			Revised Model		
	Service Quality	Satisfaction with Outcome	Job Satisfaction	Service Quality	Satisfaction with Outcome	Job Satisfaction
Communication with Service Provider						
Frequency	0.23 (7.76)	−0.05 (−1.16)	−	0.23 (8.05)	−	−
Bi-directionality	−0.05 (−1.7)	0.07 (2.0)	−	−	0.07 (2.12)	−
Communication with Manager						
Frequency	0.04 (1.43)	0.08 (2.14)	−	−	0.08 (2.42)	−
Bi-directionality	−0.11 (−3.43)	0.03 (0.8)	−	−0.11 (−3.82)	−	0.10 (2.78)
Informational Consistency	0.5 (16.79)	0.05 (1.27)	−	0.5 (16.78)	−	0.13 (3.6)
Service Quality		0.27 (6.16)	0.08 (2.26)		0.28 (8.29)	−
Satisfaction with Outcome			0.24 (6.53)			0.23 (6.65)
R^2	41%	10%	7%	41%	10%	8%
Model Fit	$\chi^2 = 15.36$; $p < 0.01$ RMSEA = 0.052 NNFI = 0.94 AGFI = 0.96			$\chi^2 = 12.55$; $p = 0.18$ RMSEA = 0.023 NNFI = 0.99 AGFI = 0.98		

Note: The numbers in the table represent standardized path coefficients (T-values)
The bold numbers represent significant paths at $p < 0.05$, 2-sided.

FIGURE 2. Revised Model: Significant Paths

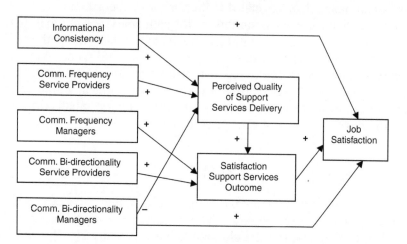

be relaxed. As shown in Table 2, the fit indices thus improved significantly. The impacted paths were the direct paths from manager's communication bi-directionality to boundary spanner's job satisfaction (t = 2.78; p < 0.01) and from informational consistency to job satisfaction (t = 3.6; p < 0.01). As implied, boundary spanners who perceive the support service delivery to be higher in quality are more satisfied with the support service outcome (t = 6.16, p < 0.01).

Regarding the hypotheses, both service quality and satisfaction with the outcomes have a significant influence on job satisfaction. However, the impact of satisfaction with the service outcome is substantially stronger (t = 6.53; p < 0.01 versus t = 2.26; p < 0.05). Moreover, when informational consistency and manager's communication bi-directionality were allowed to have a direct impact on job satisfaction, the effect of the service delivery quality on job satisfaction turned non-significant (H$_8$ supported; no support for H$_7$). These results suggest that the support services affect boundary spanners' overall job satisfaction through the environmental climate that they create. Evidently, boundary spanners who are satisfied with the resources (i.e., outcomes) provided by the support services, who feel that they have open communication channels with their managers, and those who do not experience conflicting communications, are likely to be satisfied with their job in general. As these factors only explain a small amount of the variance in job satisfaction (8%), it may seem that support services have little impact on overall job satisfaction. However, considering that the present study was limited to one support service, it is likely that the totality of the organization's support system would have a significantly greater impact on boundary spanners' overall satisfaction with their jobs. Moreover, as the study asked boundary spanners to report on their support service experience post-hoc, the service quality component's impact on job satisfaction may have been marginalized. Even with post-hoc reporting, however, 41% of the variance in service quality was explained by the communication variables. Should boundary spanners be sampled *during* a support services consumption experience, the impact on overall job satisfaction could prove to be even higher.

Concerning the effect of internal communication on boundary spanners' perceptions of service delivery quality and satisfaction with service outcomes, it is interesting to note that management communication seems to be complementary to that of the service providers. As hypothesized, service providers' communication frequency has a positive impact on perceived service delivery quality (t = 8.05; p < 0.01; H_{1b} supported) but not on satisfaction with the outcome (H_{2b} not supported). Service providers' communication bi-directionality has a positive effect on satisfaction with the service outcome (t = 2.12; p < 0.05; H_{4b} supported) but not on service delivery quality (H_{3b} not supported). It may be that boundary spanners who receive a higher volume of communication from service providers experience reduced uncertainty during the service delivery process or develop more realistic expectations of the service delivery, which serves to enhance a perception of quality service. Bi-directional communication with service providers, however, did influence satisfaction with the outcomes of the service, which may indicate negotiation toward boundary spanners' desired service benefits–akin to a customer orientation on the part of the service provider. In the context of this study, salespeople might be able to express their preferences for office location or layout and therefore end up being more satisfied with their accommodations. Hence, it is important for service providers to not only continuously inform boundary spanners about the progress made in the service delivery process, but also to maintain an open channel for two-way communication to ensure satisfaction with the end-results of the support service.

The pattern of the managers' communication effects is largely reversed. Managers' communication frequency has a positive impact on boundary spanners' satisfaction with the support service outcome (t =

2.42; $p < 0.01$; H_{2a} supported) but not on perceived service delivery quality (H_{1a} not supported). This may be explained by the idea that management's role is to specify the scope of the support services and to explain that to the boundary spanners, but management may have little involvement in the actual service delivery process itself. Managers' communication bi-directionality has an unexpected negative effect on perceived service delivery quality ($t = -3.82$; $p < 0.01$; H_{3a} refuted) and no effect on satisfaction with support service outcome (H_{4a} not supported). This result may be indicative of boundary spanners engaging in bi-directional communication with managers in order to complain about service delivery problems and seek help from managers regarding those support service issues. Hence, managers may get involved in the service delivery process only in reaction to service problems, which would explain the negative relationship. Finally, as expected, informational consistency has a very strong effect on boundary spanners' perception of the service delivery quality ($t = 16.8$; $p < 0.01$; H_5 supported) but not on their satisfaction with the service outcome (H_6 not supported). The result is not surprising given that the only component of the service providers' communication that impacted outcome satisfaction was bi-directional communication, which again could be interpreted as some level of anticipated dissatisfaction with the service. It may be that the service provider provides little (non-reciprocal) communication that explicitly addresses service outcomes; communication about services outcomes may be more exclusively the domain of managers.

IMPLICATIONS

This study was an initial attempt at empirically investigating the impact of organizational communication on boundary spanners' satisfaction with support services in organizations. In interpreting the findings of this study, it is necessary to take into consideration the study's limitations. For one, the study focused on a single support service within a single organization. Also, the firm is renowned as an industry leader in its provision of support services. While this choice enhanced the internal validity of the study by eliminating organizational and industry specific influences, additional cross-sectional research is needed to affirm the generalizability of the findings. A longitudinal study might also be revealing–to better tap satisfaction throughout the service delivery process. Further, only a limited number of communication facets have been included in the present study. Including more facets of communication might increase understanding of the communication/satisfaction relationship. In addition to communication structure elements, future studies should include constructs that better capture communication content.

Despite these limitations, the study revealed a number of important findings that help direct future research. In general, extending the conceptualization of service satisfaction, by including outcome satisfaction in addition to service quality, was revealing. It was found that service provider and manager communication with boundary spanners impacts the two satisfaction components in complementary ways. Importantly, it was found that satisfaction with service outcomes was the only satisfaction component that directly impacts overall job satisfaction. Thus, it is clear that any future research into boundary-spanning contexts should include an outcome satisfaction component in order to capture satisfaction with the end-results of the support service provision.

Specifically, future research is also needed to explain the refuted hypothesis (H3a) in which managers' bi-directional communication was found to negatively impact perceptions of service quality. Can managers play a positive role in communicating expectancies for support service delivery? Research instruments that would capture the *nature* of the bi-directional communication between managers and boundary spanners would provide a means of evaluating whether bi-directional communication could positively impact service quality. In other words, a study would be revealing of whether communication that is not "intervening" in nature (i.e., managers stepping in to mediate between the unhappy boundary spanner and the support service) aids in improving perceptions of a quality service quality.

This "mediating" role of management, between boundary spanners and support services, also hints at alternative conceptualizations of support service satisfaction. Should sales managers be considered as another important internal customer by support service providers? The extent to which sales managers understand and appreciate the services provided to salespeople may impact the way in which they communicate these services to salespeople and help mediate service-related conflicts. This in turn, might affect the appreciation and use of internal services. An extended conceptual framework that would map the dynamic between managers and service providers could prove valuable.

Finally, as customer-contact employees are in dual advocacy positions, pledging their loyalty to both customers and the organization, they often face trade-offs between satisfying customers and adhering to organizational policies. Hence, factors explored in other boundary spanning studies that describe the posture of the boundary spanner relative to the customer and firm, both physically and psychologically, such as employee-customer orientation, organizational commitment, and sales autonomy, should be included in future research. In effect, the degree to which the boundary spanner feels obligated to other value chain constituencies may moderate the impact that support service satisfaction has on job outcomes.

This research was an initial attempt to explore boundary spanner satisfaction with support services using a communications framework. It is hoped that this study has provided managerial insight into boundary spanner satisfaction with support services and has provided specific research direction to help generate more conceptual and empirical work on this important topic.

REFERENCES

Behrman, D.N., Bigoness, W.J., and Perreault, W.D., Jr. (1981). Sources of job related ambiguity and their consequences upon salesperson's job satisfaction and performance. *Management Science, 27*(4), 1246-1260.

Berry, L.L. and Parasuraman, A. (1991). *Marketing services. Competing through quality.* NY: The Free Press.

Biddle, B.J. (1979). *Role theory. Expectations, identities and behaviors.* NY: Academic Press.

Bitner, M.J. (1995). Building service relationships: it's all about promises. *Journal of the Academy of Marketing Science, 23*(4), 246-251.

Brady, M.K. and Cronin, J., Jr. (2001). Some new thoughts on conceptualizing perceived service quality: a hierarchical approach. *Journal of Marketing, 65*(3), 34-49.

Brooks, R.F., Lings, I.N., and Botschen, M.A. (1999). Internal marketing and customer driven wavefronts. *The Service Industries Journal, 19*(4), 49-67.

Brown, S.P. and Peterson, R.A. (1994). The effect of effort on sales performance and job satisfaction. *Journal of Marketing, 58*(2), 70-82.

Burrows, P. (2001). The era of efficiency. *Business Week*, June 18.

Cronin, J., Jr. and Taylor, S.A. (1992). Measuring service quality: a reexamination and extension. *Journal of Marketing, 56*(3), 55-68.

Crosby, L.A., Evans, K.R. and Cowles, D. (1990). Relationship quality in services selling: an interpersonal influence perspective. *Journal of Marketing, 54*(3), 68-80.

Davis, T.R.V. (1991). Internal service operations: strategies for increasing their effectiveness and controlling their costs. *Organizational Dynamics, 20*, 5-22.

Dubinsky, A.J., Howell, R.D., Ingram, T.N. and Bellenger, D.N. (1986). Salesforce socialization. *Journal of Marketing, 50*(4), 192-207.

Edvardsson, B. and Gustavsson, B. (1991). Quality in services and quality in service organizations: a model of quality assessment. In S. Brown, E. Gummesson,

B. Edvardsson and B. Gustavsson (eds.), *Service quality: multidisciplinary and multinational perspectives.* Lexington, MA: Lexington Books, 319-340.

Evans, K.R., Gremler, D.D., Schlachter, J.L. and Wolfe, W.G. (1995). The impact of salesperson socialization on organizational commitment, satisfaction, and performance in a professional service organization. *Journal of Professional Services Marketing, 11*(2), 139-157.

_____, Arnold, T.J., Grant, J.A. (1999). Combining service and sales at the point of customer contact. *Journal of Service Research, 2*(1), 34-49.

Finn, D.W., Baker, J., Marshall, G.W. and Anderson, R. (1996). Total quality management and internal customers: measuring internal service quality. *Journal of Marketing Theory and Practice, 4*(3), 36-51.

Fisher, R.J., Maltz, E. and Jaworski, B.J. (1997). Enhancing communication between marketing and engineering: the moderating role of relative functional identification. *Journal of Marketing, 61*(3), 54-70.

George, W. (1990). Internal marketing and organizational behavior: a partnership in developing customer-conscious employees at every level. *Journal of Business Research, 20*(1), 63-70.

Gremler, D.D., Bitner, M.J. and Evans, K.R. (1994). The internal service encounter. *International Journal of Service Industry Management, 5*(2), 34-56.

Gronroos, C. (1985). Internal marketing: theory and practice. In T. Bloch, G. Upah, and V. Zeithaml (eds.), *Services marketing in a changing environment.* Chicago: American Marketing Association, 41-47.

Gummesson, E. (1987). Using internal marketing to develop a new culture–the case of Ericsson quality. *Journal of Business and Industrial Marketing, 2*(3), 23-28.

Hartline, M.D., Maxham, J.G. III, McKee, D.O. (2000). Corridors of influence in the dissemination of customer-oriented strategy to customer contact service employees. *Journal of Marketing, 64*(2), 35-50.

Hays, R.D. (1996). The strategic power of internal service excellence. *Business-Horizons*, July-August, 15-20.

Heskett, J.L., Jones, T.O., Loveman, G.W., Sasser, Jr., W.E. and Schlesinger, L.A. (1994). Putting the service-profit chain to work. *Harvard Business Review*, March-April, 164-174.

Holbrook, M.B. (1994). The nature of customer value. An axiology of services in the consumption experience. In R.T. Rust and R.L. Oliver (eds.), *Service quality. New directions in theory and practice.* Thousand Oaks, CA: SAGE Publications.

Jablin, F.M. (1982). Organizational communication: an assimilation approach. In M.E. Roloff and C.R. Berger (eds.), *Social cognition and communication.* Newbury Park, CA: Sage, 255-286.

_____ (1987). Organizational entry, assimilation and exit. In Frederic M. Jablin, Linda L. Putnam, Karlene H. Roberts and Lyman W. Porter (eds.), *Handbook of organizational communication.* Newbury Park, CA: Sage Publications, Inc.

Jacobs, R. S., Evans, K.R., Kleine, R.E., and Landry, T.D. (2001). Disclosure and its reciprocity as predictors of key outcomes of an initial sales encounter. *Journal of Personal Selling and Sales Management, 21*(1), 51-62.

Johlke, M.C. and Duhan, D.F. (2000). Supervisor communication practices and service employee job outcomes. *Journal of Service Research, 3*(2), 154-166.

Katz, D. and Kahn, R.L. (1966). *The social psychology of organizations*. NY: John Wiley & Sons Inc.

Kelley, S.W., Donnelly, Jr., J.H. and Skinner, S. (1990). Customer participation in service production and delivery. *Journal of Retailing, 66*(3), 315-335.

_____, Skinner, S.J. and Donnelly, J.H. (1992). Organizational socialization of service customers. *Journal of Business Research, 25*, 197-214.

Lovelock, C. (1991). *Services marketing*, 2nd ed. Englewood Cliffs, NJ: Prentice Hall.

Mills, P.K. and Morris, J.H. (1986). Clients as 'partial' employees of service organizations: role development in client participation. *Academy of Management Review, 11*, 726-735.

_____ and Ungson, G.R. (2001). Internal market structures; substitutes for hierarchies. *Journal of Service Research, 3*(3), 252-264.

Mohr, J.J. and Nevin, J. (1990). Communication strategies in marketing channels: a theoretical perspective. *Journal of Marketing, 50*(4), 36-51.

_____ and Sohi, R.S. (1995). Communication flows in distribution channels: impact on assessments of communication quality and satisfaction. *Journal of Retailing, 71*(4), 393-416.

_____, Fisher, R.J. and Nevin, J.R. (1996). Collaborative communication in interfirm relationships: moderating effects of integration and control. *Journal of Marketing, 60*(3), 103-115.

Nagel, P.J.A. and W.W. Cilliers (1990). Customer satisfaction: a comprehensive approach. *International Journal of Physical Distribution and Logistics, 20*(6), 2-46.

Parasuraman, A., Zeithaml, V.A., and Berry, L.L. (1985). A conceptual model of service quality and its implications for future research. *Journal of Marketing, 49* (Fall), 41-50.

_____, Zeithaml, V.A., and Berry, L.L. (1988). SERVQUAL: a multiple-item scale for measuring consumer perceptions of service quality. *Journal of Retailing, 64*(1), 12-37.

Rafiq, M. and Ahmed, P.K. (1995). The limits of internal marketing. In P. Kunst and J. Lemmink (eds.), *Managing service quality*. London: Paul Chapman Publishing, 121-132.

_____ and Ahmed, P.K. (2000). Advances in the internal marketing concept: definition, synthesis and extension. *Journal of Services Marketing, 14*(6), 449-462.

Ruekert, R. and Walker, O.C., Jr. (1987). Marketing's interaction with other functional units: a conceptual framework and empirical evidence. *Journal of Marketing, 51*(1), 1-19.

Rust, R.T. and Oliver, R.L. (1994). Service quality. Insights and managerial implications from the frontier. In R.T. Rust and R.L. Oliver (eds.), *Service quality. New directions for theory and practice*. Thousand Oaks, CA: SAGE Publications.

_____, Stewart, G.L., Miller, H. and Pielack, D. (1996). The satisfaction and retention of frontline employees: a customer satisfaction measurement approach. *International Journal of Service Industry Management, 7*(5), 62-80.

Schneider, B. and Bowen, D.E. (1995). *Winning the service game*. Boston: Harvard Press.

_____, White, S.S. and Paul, M.C. (1998). Linking service climate and customer perceptions of service quality: test of a causal model. *Journal of Applied Psychology, 83*(2), 150-163.

Sergeant, A. and Frenkel, S. (2000). When do customer contact employees satisfy customers? *Journal of Service Research, 3*(1), 18-34.

Solomon, M.R., Surprenant, C., Czepiel, J.A. and Gutman, E.G. (1985). A role theory perspective on dyadic interactions: the service encounter. *Journal of Marketing, 49*(4), 99-111.

Stauss, B. (1995). Internal services: classification and quality management. *International Journal of Service Industry Management, 6*(2), 62-78.

Stohl, C. and Redding, W.C. (1987). Messages and message exchange processes. In F. Jablin et al. (eds.), *Handbook of organization communication.* Newbury Park, CA: Sage, 451-502.

Teas, K.R. (1983). Supervisory behavior, role stress, and the job satisfaction of industrial salespeople. *Journal of Marketing Research, 20*(1), 84-91.

Wetzler, M., de Ruyter, K., and Lemmink, J. (1999). Role stress and after-sales service management. *Journal of Service Research, 2*(1), 50-67.

Williams, K.C. and Spiro, R.L. (1985). Communication style in the salesperson-customer dyad. *Journal of Marketing Research, 22*(4), 434-42.

A Conceptualization
of the Employee Branding Process

Sandra Jeanquart Miles

Murray State University

Glynn Mangold

Murray State University

Sandra Jeanquart Miles, DBA, SPHR, is Professor of Management, Department of Management, Marketing and Business Administration, College of Business and Public Affairs, Murray State University, Murray, KY 42071 (E-mail: sandy.miles@ murraystate.edu). Dr. Miles is certified as a Senior Professional of Human Resources by the Human Resource Certification Institute. She has published many articles pertaining to human resource issues and supervisory and subordinate relations. Dr. Miles has also held several leadership positions in the Midwest Academy of Management and the Society for Human Resource Management.

Glynn Mangold, PhD, is Professor of Marketing, Department of Management, Marketing and Business Administration, College of Business and Public Affairs, Murray State University, Murray, KY 42071 (E-mail: glynn.mangold@murraystate.edu). While much of his research has focused on the marketing of services, Dr. Mangold's academic interests are diverse with over thirty peer-reviewed publications to his credit. He has served as Editor of the *Journal of Business and Public Affairs*, Electronic Resources Editor for *Marketing Education Review*, and is a member of the editorial review boards for a number of journals.

The authors would like to express appreciation to the guest editor and the anonymous reviewers for their contributions to the manuscript. Its quality was greatly enhanced by their efforts.

[Haworth co-indexing entry note]: "A Conceptualization of the Employee Branding Process." Miles, Sandra Jeanquart, and Glynn Mangold. Co-published simultaneously in *Journal of Relationship Marketing* (Best Business Books, an imprint of The Haworth Press, Inc.) Vol. 3, No. 2/3, 2004, pp. 65-87; and: *Internal Relationship Management: Linking Human Resources to Marketing Performance* (ed: Michael D. Hartline, and David Bejou) Best Business Books, an imprint of The Haworth Press, Inc., 2004, pp. 65-87. Single or multiple copies of this article are available for a fee from The Haworth Document Delivery Service [1-800-HAWORTH, 9:00 a.m. - 5:00 p.m. (EST). E-mail address: docdelivery@haworthpress.com].

SUMMARY. We propose a conceptual model of the employee branding process in which the employee brand image is driven by the messages employees receive and the mechanisms within employees' psyches that enable them to make sense of those messages. The model identifies various sources through which messages are delivered and describes the contributions of those sources to the employee branding process. The psychological contract is identified as a perceptual mechanism central to the employee branding process. The model specifies the consequences of the employee branding process and describes a feedback loop through which managers can monitor the process. *[Article copies available for a fee from The Haworth Document Delivery Service: 1-800-HAWORTH. E-mail address: <docdelivery@haworthpress.com> Website: <http://www.HaworthPress.com>*

KEYWORDS. Employee branding, internal marketing, psychological contracts

Organizations use brands to give their offerings an identity and to distinguish them from competitive offerings. These brands typically take the form of words, signs, symbols, or designs. Employees, too, can reinforce, strengthen, and even create a brand image for their products and organizations. Employee brand-building behaviors may include courtesy, responsiveness, reliability, helpfulness, and empathy, among others. Such behaviors have been shown to contribute to consumers' perceptions of service quality and may result in higher levels of customer retention and loyalty (American Society for Quality Control, 1988; Parasuraman, Zeithaml, & Berry, 1985; Parasuraman, Zeithaml, & Berry, 1988).

For instance, Southwest Airlines employees have established and reinforced that firm's image as a fun, upbeat organization that makes an extra effort to ensure that its customers and employees are satisfied (Freiberg & Freiberg, 1996). According to Brown (2003), not only does Southwest have satisfied customers and employees; it has satisfied investors as well. One of the company's press releases notes that Southwest is the only airline that has posted profits for 30 consecutive years and paid dividends for 106 consecutive quarters (Southwest Airline, 2003). These successes have come at a time when other airlines have been struggling for mere survival.

It is important to understand how organizations can succeed in their quest to have employees deliver a service experience that is consistent with both customer expectations and the brand image desired by the organization. Because these service experiences can only be delivered by the employees who represent the organization, the task of getting employees to reflect the organization's brand image and deliver on its promises is a challenge for businesses. Recently, employee branding has garnered managerial and research attention that focuses on addressing this challenge. Employee branding has been conceptualized in a number of ways (Estell, 2002; Farrell, 2002; Frook, 2001; McKenzie, 2001; Mitchell, 2002). While each conceptualization recognizes the importance of employee branding and its positive outcomes, there is little agreement on exactly what employee branding is or how it happens. Therefore, the employee branding construct itself appears to be underconceptualized.

The purpose of this article is to present a comprehensive model for understanding the employee branding process. We give attention to the definition of employee branding, the sources of messages employees receive, the factors that influence employee perceptions, and, ultimately, the development of an employee brand image. We also address the positive consequences likely to accrue from effective employee branding efforts.

THE DEFINITION AND CONCEPTUAL CONTEXT OF EMPLOYEE BRANDING

Successful product branding strategies focus on the image organizations create in the minds of their customers regarding their products. This image-creation process focuses largely on external communications with customers and customers' personal experiences with the organization's products. The idea of branding and the development of brand equity has been applied to intangible services as well as tangible products (Krishnan & Hartline, 2001). This traditional view of the branding process provides one backdrop for the conceptualization of employee branding, but employee branding is also rooted in the practice of internal marketing.

As Rafiq and Ahmed (2000) point out, various lines of thought underpin the concept of internal marketing. First, internal marketing has been seen as a process by which marketing tools and techniques can be used to motivate employees to achieve the organization's goals and objectives, particularly as they relate to interactions with external customers (Gronroos, 1981). Employees have also been seen as internal customers, and achieving employee satisfaction has been viewed as a key to having satisfied external customers (Berry, 1981; George, 1977). The emphasis on internal customers has led to the suggestion that their needs should be satisfied through the "job-products" the organization offers (Berry & Parasuraman, 1991, p. 151). Finally, internal marketing has been seen as a device by which organizational change can be accomplished and strategies implemented (Rafiq & Ahmed, 1993; Winter, 1985). Rafiq and Ahmed's (2000) careful review of the literature led them to propose the following definition of internal marketing:

> Internal marketing is a planned effort using a marketing-like approach . . . to overcome organizational resistance to change and to align, motivate and interfunctionally co-ordinate and integrate . . . employees towards the effective implementation of corporate and functional strategies . . . in order to deliver customer satisfaction . . . through a process of creating motivated and customer orientated employees. (p. 454)

The definition of internal marketing proposed by Rafiq and Ahmed (2000) focuses on using a marketing-like approach to get internal customers (i.e., employees) to deliver satisfaction to the organization's external customers. However, employee branding goes beyond attaining customer satisfaction through internal marketing. It utilizes all the organizational systems, including internal marketing methods, to motivate employees to project the desired organizational image. This image is projected through their demeanor, appearance, and manner of interacting with customers.

Employees must effectively internalize the desired image before they can project it to others (Joseph, 1996; Reardon & Enis, 1990). This brand internalization process comes about, in part, when employees receive messages from the various systems internal to the organization. When the messages are consistent and credible, the internalization process enables employees to better fulfill the explicit and implicit promises inherent in the brand name and organizational image (Greene, Walls, & Schrest, 1994). Thus, we define employee branding as *the process by which employees internalize the desired brand image and are motivated to project the image to customers and other organizational constituents.*

Internal marketing initiatives traditionally have targeted boundary-spanning employees because they are the point of contact between the organization and various stakeholder groups such as the customer (Katz & Kahn, 1978). However, employee branding efforts should also focus on employees who provide direct and indirect support to the boundary-spanning function, since the boundary spanners are their internal customers (Frost & Kumar, 2000). Employees who provide direct support to the boundary-spanning function include clerical and technical support people, as well as those who provide information to the boundary spanners. Indirect support for the boundary-spanning function comes from the product or service producers who are the ultimate source of quality. Frost and Kumar (2000) found both sets of employees to be pivotal in delivering service quality. Given this finding, a comprehensive organizational approach is integral to our model of employee branding.

The image the organization projects to customers and other relevant stakeholders through its employees is the central component of successful employee branding. The projected image may pertain to the organization as a whole, to specific products and service offerings, or to both. To be successful at employee branding, organizations must create and instill the desired image in employees' minds before the image can be projected from the employees to others. Therefore, it is necessary to have a clear understanding of the most basic relationship in the organization–the relationship between the employer and the employee.

When people join organizations, a psychological contract is established between them and their employers (Rousseau, 1995). In essence, this contract is based on the employees' perceptions of a series of established expectations. For instance, employees may perceive that the organization expects them to give forth their best effort, have organizational loyalty, and work toward organizational goals. Simultaneously, employees may expect the organization to be caring, to be fair in dealing with them, to provide rewards commensurate with performance, and to offer them opportunities to develop and advance within the system. It is important to note that the organization must meet employees' expectations if it expects to fulfill its end of the perceived contract (Rousseau, 1995).

Organizational values and the desired organizational image can be transferred to employees through effective management of employees' psychological contracts. This transfer takes place through various message sources. For example, the organization's desired level of customer orientation is one value-based image that may be transferred to employees. The effective transfer of the desired customer orientation hinges on two points. First, the organization must communicate its values and expectations to employees as they pertain to customer orientation. Second, employees must perceive that the employer is delivering on its end of the psychological contract by meeting the employees' expectations. The contractual nature of the employer-employee relationship suggests that the extent to which employees display the desired customer orientation will be driven by the employees' perceptions of the extent to which the organization is delivering on its part of the psychological contract.

THE EMPLOYEE BRANDING PROCESS

As indicated in Figure 1, the psychological contract emanates from the messages employees receive. These messages form the basis of the psychological contract. They also influence the perception of the exchange relationship over time as the employee interprets and compares new messages for consistency with the psychological contract. The psychological contract drives the brand image exhibited by employees. Possible consequences of successful employee branding efforts include reduced turnover, increased employee satisfaction and performance, enhanced service quality, and a higher level of customer retention.

FIGURE 1. A Conceptualization of the Employee Branding Process

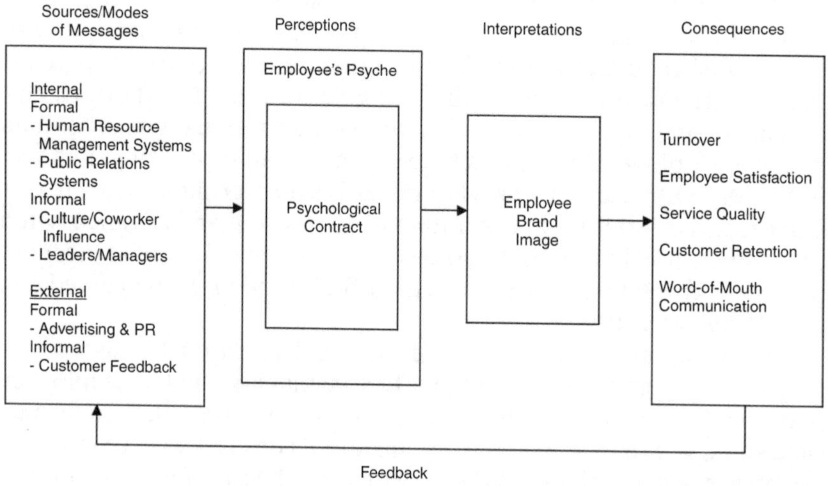

Sources/Modes of Messages

For managers seeking to establish a positive employee brand, it is important to consider that the images employees project are derived from numerous sources both within and outside the organization. The formal and informal sources of information that are internal to the organization will be addressed first, followed by a discussion of various external formal and informal sources.

The internal sources presented in Figure 1 consist of the messages generated by human resource systems and promotional and public relations systems within the organization, by organizational culture and coworker influence, and by management. Evidence indicates that it is important that the messages generated within the system be consistent (Greene, Walls, & Schrest, 1994). In reality, however, the messages are often badly mismatched (Mitchell, 2002). When different messages are delivered to employees and customers, employees who are privy to both messages will perceive a certain level of duplicity on the part of the organization. Employees will be less likely to make the necessary emotional connection with the brand and, therefore, will be less likely to deliver on the organization's promises (Robinson, 1996). This failure to deliver on promises undermines the organization's external communications programs from the employees' perspective. Therefore, the messages in the organizational system are pivotal to effective employee branding efforts.

Formal Internal Sources

The formal sources of information that are internal to the firm include the human resource management and public relations systems. These systems can be highly effective in the employee branding process for two reasons. First, managers can exert a high degree of control over both systems. Second, the messages generated by these systems can emotionally connect employees to both the brand and the organization.

Human Resource Management Systems. Human resource management systems ensure the effective and efficient use of human resources (Mathis & Jackson, 2000). Therefore, the attraction and retention of employees whose performance is consistent with organizational goals is a top priority for human resource managers (Jones & George, 2003). A strategic approach to the human resource management effort dictates that the messages emanating from the system be consistent with each other, as well as with other elements of the organizational architecture.

Huselid, Jackson, and Schuler (1997) underscored the importance of the human resource management effort when they found that effectiveness in this area positively affected organizational productivity, financial performance, and stock market values. Other evidence suggests that excellence in human resource management may constitute a core competency that leads to competitive advantage (Gratton, 1998; Hamel & Prahalad, 1994). This competitive advantage is achieved through the processes of attracting and retaining employees, training and development, and compensating employees in equitable ways. The messages inherent in these processes have a large influence on the formation and maintenance of employee expectations. Thus, it is important that the messages within the human resource management system be consistent with one another and with the organization's other messages (Goetting, 2000).

During the recruiting and staffing phases, employees start to gather information about the organization and job in which they are interested. This information may be gathered from various sources. Formal internal sources of information about the organization include recruitment documents, newspapers and periodicals, and the organization's Internet sites. Other information can be gleaned from messages sent to external constituents. Information about job responsibilities derives from a number of sources, including previous experience, education, job descriptions and specifications, and organizational contacts. Once employees are on board, a great deal of additional information about the job and organization can be gleaned from contacts within the organization. The initial gathering of information helps employees understand the goals and values of the organization and begin to form expectations about what life will be like in the organization.

As the recruitment and selection stage progresses, applicants have a choice to self-select out if the goals and values of the organization are not consistent with their own goals and values. If they choose to continue the process, the information gathered results in a set of exchange expectations that continue to form as new information is received. Much of this new information is gathered from the messages sent throughout the selection process. For example, organizations wanting to instill a customer-oriented image or brand may focus much of the communication surrounding the recruiting and staffing process on the importance of proper attitude.

Training and development are also important in terms of the messages employees receive. Training helps employees to master skills and glean knowledge required for their immediate job, while development is geared toward increasing employees' skills, knowledge, or behaviors, with the goal of improving their ability to meet changing job requirements (Noe et al., 2003). Thus, training and development are key features in a learning organization (Gephart et al., 1996). Employee expectations also evolve as a result of the message-sending process that occurs in training and development. It is, therefore, important that the messages sent in the training and development process be consistent with those sent in the recruitment process. For example, training and development activities that focus on developing the organization's brand image as it relates to customer orientation may send various messages about the customer service behavior the organization expects employees to exhibit.

Compensation is another powerful tool for aligning employee interests with organizational goals. Pay influences employee attitudes and behaviors, and it influences the kinds of individuals who are attracted to and remain with an organization (Noe et al., 2003). The link between performance and reward sends strong messages about what the organization feels is important. It also provides the basis for employee expectations (Vroom, 1964). For example, employees may have been told that promotions and raises are based largely on the degree of their customer orientation. Those who display a high level of customer orientation but do not receive the promised raises or promotions are likely to perceive that their expectations have not been met. Frustration, low performance levels, and employee turnover may result, particularly if the employees perceive that coworkers who are less customer oriented are getting the same or more rewards (Adams, 1963).

Performance management is the means through which managers align employee activities congruently with the goals of the organization (Noe et al., 2003). Performance management systems go beyond performance appraisals by providing employees with specific criteria related to organizational expectations for performance. They also measure performance and provide specific performance-related feedback to employees.

Again, the messages received through the performance management system must be consistent with organizational strategy and the other messages in the system. This specific and consistent information contributes to the employees' understanding of what they are doing or not doing well and helps to identify areas in which improvement is needed. In the absence of such information, employees tend to assume they are doing a good job and continue at their current performance levels. In some cases, these employees are surprised when their annual evaluations indicate substandard performance, particularly when their pay raises are influenced by the evaluation. These employees are likely to feel that they have not received procedural justice and that the initial promises made during recruitment and selection have been breached (Folger & Konovsky, 1989). On the other hand, employees who fail to perform and yet receive favorable evaluations may come to the conclusion that performance doesn't matter. Under either scenario, inconsistent messages result in suboptimal results for the organization.

In summary, the messages sent through human resource policies and practices tell employees what the organization values or deems important. High levels of message consistency help clarify the employees' understanding of how the organization expects them to behave.

Public Relations Systems. An organization can use public relations to influence its image and the image of its products and services (Kerin et al., 2003). In the context of employee branding, public relations efforts should be targeted to employees, as well as external constituents. For instance, an organization may want to use public relations to create the impression that it is customer oriented. Yet, if rigid corporate policies limit the extent to which employees can provide good service, these conflicting messages may result in confusion about the organization's values and produce an overall lack of trust.

Internal public relations efforts can also be enhanced when organizations target employees with their advertising. Advertising messages can enable employees to better understand the product brand image and increase their emotional connection to that image (Mitchell, 2002). For instance, when Carly Fiorina became CEO of Hewlett-Packard, the company's new advertising campaign targeted employees as well as external constituents. The campaign, titled "Invent," featured the garage where Bill Hewlett and Dave Packard created their first inventions. Ms. Fiorina was featured in the campaign along with the following message: "The original start-up will act like one again." A surge of energy was unleashed throughout the organization as the campaign caught on (Mitchell, 2002). In this and similar cases, the employees' strong emotional connections with the brand can make the brand image more vivid to customers, thereby fulfilling and reinforcing customer expectations.

Informal Internal Sources

Informal internal sources of messages can consist of interactions with or observations of employees, supervisors, and friends who work for the company. These interactions and observations are often viewed as part of the informal socialization process (Allen & Meyer, 1990) because they help employees adjust to their jobs and learn the ropes of the organization. The influence of coworkers, as well as the organization's culture, leadership, and management, plays an important role in employee branding.

Coworker Influence. Any interaction with or observation of employees who are not acting in their official capacity at the time of the communication falls into the category of informal communications. Informal communications can occur with anyone in the organization, including human resource managers, supervisors, and coworkers.

The information transmitted through coworkers may sometimes reflect organizational realities more accurately than the information transmitted through formal sources. For example, an individual may base his or her decision to join an organization on formal written documentation provided as part of the recruitment process. This documentation may indicate that financial rewards are based on the degree of customer orientation an employee shows. However, after joining the organization the employee may hear through informal socialization processes that raises typically constitute a straight percentage of salary and are given out across the board. At year's end, the information transmitted through the informal channel may be confirmed by the amount of the raises and their recipients. In these instances, an employee is likely to call into question the integrity of the formal sources of the messages or, even worse, of the organization as a whole.

Influence of the Organization's Culture. The organizational culture constitutes another informal internal source of information. Organizational culture consists of a set of values, norms, standards of behavior, and common expectations that control the manner in which individuals and groups interact and work to achieve organizational goals (Jones & George, 2003). Organizational values and norms send messages to members about what goals they should pursue and how they should behave to reach those goals (Jones & George, 2003). These messages may or may not be consistent with the stated goals of the organization and the messages received through formal organizational sources.

Mixed messages are sent to employees when the organization's norms, values, and standards of behavior conflict with other organizational systems. In such situations, the transfer of values and assumptions takes place through a socialization process. Employees receiving mixed messages may sometimes feel that the organization lacks integrity and consequently may act in ways that are inconsistent with the organization's best interests.

The corporate culture can be reinforced or perpetuated through reward systems (Ott, 1989). These systems are typically incorporated into the firm's evaluation and compensation systems and thus can be used to further corporate values. For instance, organizations wishing to instill an employee branding image that reflects a strong customer orientation may use awards or contests to reward those who display outstanding customer-service behaviors.

Influence of Organizational Leadership and Management. The employee socialization process is largely driven by the messages an organization's leaders and managers transmit to employees. Leadership is the influence a person exerts over other people to inspire, motivate, and direct their activities to achieve organizational goals (Yukl, 1989). Kelman (1958) indicated that people could be influenced by compliance, identification, internalization, or some combination of the three. Compliance occurs when people do something against their will because of coercion. People obey in this type of system because of the high costs of disobedience. For example, employees may not be willing to argue the benefits of a new program with a supervisor because they may believe that such arguments may negatively impact their careers. Identification occurs when people do things leaders want them to do because they like them and want to help them accomplish their objectives. While this generates positive behavior while the leader is present, such behavior may cease if the organization's leadership changes. For this reason, this type of leadership style does not lend itself well to helping employees permanently internalize the brand image and deliver on its promises.

Internalization occurs when followers are convinced that acting in a particular way, as directed by their leaders, is in both their own and the organization's best interest. Values and opinions are internalized when employees place a great deal of trust in their leaders' judgment and expertise or when employees accept the logic of their leaders' thinking. Such employees tend to be highly motivated and effective. Leaders who successfully enable employees to internalize the organization's values are viewed as charismatic or transformational leaders and can influence change through vision, intellectual stimulation, and acknowledgment of the differences among subordinates. Typically, they help their subordinates understand the organization's values and vision and are able to communicate a plan for achieving the vision (Burns, 1978).

Managers can either convey messages in the same way as the organization's leaders or through interpretation of organizational policies. For instance, an organization may state a strong commitment to customer-service training and development. However, if individual managers are more concerned about immediate production and bottom-line numbers, they may discourage employees from–or even penalize them for–using work time to attend training and development programs. Additionally, conflicting messages within organizations may lead to confusion about what behaviors employees should exhibit. Employees who receive conflicting messages are likely to become frustrated and begin questioning the organization's integrity. In such circumstances, the organization's culture, leaders, and managers aid in the socialization process by signaling to employees what the organization is really after despite the formal messages received. Employees are less likely to be confused when an organization's leaders and managers deliver informal messages that are consistent with the formal messages employees receive about the organization.

Formal External Sources

Formal external sources of messages include advertising and public relations. These sources transmit information about the organization and brand image to a broad range of external constituents, including customers and stockholders. Employees are often secondary recipients of such external messages.

Public Relations. External public relations efforts often focus on the building of brand images for organizations, as well as the products and services they offer (Kotler, 2003). Public relations efforts can be used to either create or strengthen a positive image of the company or to alter negative images associated with problems or crises. However, employees may sense duplicity on the part of the organization when a conflict between real goals versus stated goals becomes obvious (Robbins, 1994). For instance, a company wanting to portray itself as being customer oriented may influence public opinion by creating commercials and advertisements depicting high levels of customer service. If such messages are found to be inconsistent with company operations, however, the employees' level of trust in the organization may be diminished. They may also become confused about the organization's true values and its expectations for employee behavior. For instance, a health care organization may try to create an image of caring for its patients by spending millions of dollars on a public relations campaign. At the same time, it may reward its workers for cutting costs, which may impact quality care. These mixed signals can decrease employees' trust in the organization and call its true values into question.

Advertising. Advertising also sends messages about what the organization considers to be important. For example, consider again the health care organization that advertises patient welfare as its primary concern while telling its employees that cost reduction is the organization's top priority. Such a conflict between real goals versus stated goals can undermine the firm's integrity as perceived by its employees (Mitchell, 2002; Robbins, 1994). A perceived lack of integrity affects the employees' trust in and loyalty to the organization, as well as their willingness and ability to project a positive brand image and deliver on the company's promises. To have satisfied customers, an organization must first have satisfied employees (Gronroos, 1981; Heskett & Jones, 1994).

Messages sent to external constituencies have to be consistent with the messages sent to internal constituencies, whether the organization uses public relations and advertising to create and maintain an image or whether it uses them to downplay problems or crises. An organization's integrity is at stake in the eyes of its employees when it delivers inconsistent messages.

Informal External Sources

Informal communications from external sources often come in the form of customer feedback and word-of-mouth communication from friends and acquaintances. Such communication can have a significant impact on employees' psyches. For example, customer-oriented employees may feel that their outstanding efforts to ensure customer satisfaction are consistent with organizational values as well as the organizational reward system. However, should those employees hear stories from friends and acquaintances about poor customer service, they may question the organization's true level of customer orientation. Should the stories pertain to actions by those in higher levels of management, their questioning may become more intense and may even engender a feeling of betrayal.

The above example illustrates the affect that word-of-mouth communication from external sources can have on employees' thought processes. In fact, the influence of word-of-mouth communications in general should not be underestimated, whether its source is internal or external to the organization. Word-of-mouth communication is highly credible, compared to the organization's formal communications and the messages that come through media advertising (Bone, 1995; Herr,

Kardes, & Kim, 1991), resulting in a substantial affect on employees' expectations, attitudes, and perceptions of fairness.

In summary, the messages within the organizational system communicate information about the organization's operations, values, and goals, as well as its brand image. However, the number of messages in the system is enormous. As employees take these messages in, they are processed and monitored for content as well as consistency. This monitoring process forms the basis for the employees' understanding of what the organization expects of them in exchange for their efforts.

PSYCHOLOGICAL CONTRACT

The psychological contract between the organization and employees is based on a series of expectations established between the organization and its employees. The expectations are based on messages employees receive about the organization beginning with the recruitment process and lasting throughout their tenure with the firm. The more realistic and consistent the messages, the less likely it is that the contract will be violated. As long as the contract is honored, employees will believe in and trust the organization because it has delivered on its promises (Robinson, 1996). On the other hand, if employees feel that the psychological contract has been violated, they will experience negative feelings and engage in behaviors that are not in the best interest of the organization (Robinson & Rousseau, 1994). Negative outcomes associated with perceived violations of the psychological contract include diminished loyalty, negative word-of-mouth communication directed to other employees and even customers, reduced productivity, and employee turnover (Robinson & Rousseau, 1994; Rousseau, 1995).

The employees determine whether the psychological contract has been violated and whether the organization can be trusted. Assume, for example, that employees receive initial messages suggesting that the organization places a high value on customer satisfaction and that it will treat its employees in the same way that employees are expected to treat customers. This message forms a set of employee expectations pertaining to the respect and fairness with which they will be treated. It also sets a standard for the treatment of the organization's customers. Messages consistent with the organization's commitment to customer and employee satisfaction should emanate throughout the system in such areas as performance evaluation, compensation, and job responsibilities.

The result should produce a high level of customer service as well as satisfied employees.

When employees see inconsistencies in the organization, they may scrutinize further transactions in their part of the organization to reassure themselves that their contract is still intact and that the organization can be trusted. For example, if an organization is being investigated for potential truth-in-advertising violations, even those employees who are not affected by the investigation are likely to more fully examine all of the incoming messages for consistency or inconsistency. Ensuring the consistency of all organizational messages may seem an impossible task. Fortunately, however, some violations of the psychological contract appear to go unnoticed by employees if the organization appears to be fulfilling the majority of the contract on a regular basis (Rousseau, 1995).

The psychological contract is pivotal to building the employee brand image. It is only when an organization understands and uses the psychological contract to establish expectations for employee behavior that employees understand what is expected and how they can meet those expectations. The messages emanating from the organizational system influence the employees' perceptions of the importance of customer service or other organizational values. Employees will have a stronger customer-service orientation when the information in the system frequently and consistently reinforces those messages (Mitchell, 2002). For instance, formal human resource management systems may communicate messages such as the following: (1) the company only hires friendly people, (2) the company commits resources to training employees on customer service and product knowledge, and (3) the company rewards employees for outstanding customer service.

These messages can communicate the organization's customer-service expectations and form the basis for employees' degree of customer orientation. However, the most effective delivery of customer service requires that employees internalize the organization's customer service messages. This internalization process will better enable employees to base their job-related decisions and behaviors on the organization's brand image and to project that image to customers (Mitchell, 2002). Higher levels of internalization can be expected when the organization's external and internal messages are consistent and frequently delivered.

The process of internalization enables employees to better understand customers' needs, wants, and expectations, as well as the organization's customer service standards. Such increased understanding can be expected to lead to higher levels of customer orientation.

EMPLOYEE BRAND IMAGE

The development of employee brands is driven by the degree to which employees internalize the organization's brand image and are motivated to project that image to customers and other organizational constituents. The internalization of the desired brand image occurs best when employees feel a high level of trust in the organization for which they work. The fulfillment of employees' psychological contracts with the organization is critical to the process of developing high levels of employee trust.

When employees perceive that the organization has broken its promises to them, they may also question whether it will fulfill its promises to customers. Consequently, employees may feel reluctant to promise something to customers that may not be delivered. When this occurs, the feeling of trust has been broken, the brand image is somewhat compromised, and employees may not deliver desired levels of customer service. On the other hand, if employees perceive that their psychological contracts have been upheld, they are likely to view the organization as delivering on its promises. Under such circumstances, employees are likely to fulfill organizational expectations by projecting a positive brand image and delivering high levels of customer service.

CONSEQUENCES

Several favorable consequences are likely to accrue to organizations in which a strong brand image is developed. They are likely to benefit from higher levels of employee satisfaction and performance, service quality, and customer retention, as well as reduced employee turnover (Rousseau, 1995). In addition, customers who perceive strong brand images may be more likely to engage in favorable word-of-mouth communication. Employees may also be more likely to engage in favorable word-of-mouth communication when they feel their psychological contracts have been fulfilled. The messages these satisfied employees send may go to other current and prospective employees, as well as to the organization's current and future customers.

Inconsistent messages threaten or nullify the psychological contract, resulting in negative perceptions and attitudes. Violations of the psychological contract may well cause employees to leave because they have a negative impact on employees' trust and satisfaction (Robinson & Rousseau, 1994). Negative word-of-mouth communications may also result, which have an unfavorable impact on those who hear the messages. Acts of workplace sabotage have even been linked to perceived violations of the psychological contract (Paul & Niehoff, 2000).

FEEDBACK

The feedback loop allows managers to assess the quality of the employee branding system. Employee turnover is measurable through the organization's human resource system and customer retention can be gauged through metrics used in the organization's marketing information system. Additionally, validated scales are typically available for the measurement of employee and customer satisfaction and customer perceptions of service quality. Although managers may not be able to quickly identify changes in employees' perceptions and attitudes, they can usually observe employees' behavior in which the perceptions and attitudes are manifested. Undesirable behavior can often be traced either to the messages the organization sends or to the channels through which the messages are sent.

When an indicator such as customer satisfaction drops, investigation into the causes may warrant additional research. For example, banks that experience high levels of customer turnover sometimes conduct employee climate surveys to provide insight into the reasons for customer defection. Underlying organizational issues, such as employees' inattention to customer needs and preferences, are then explored. When necessary, organizational messages can be adjusted to remedy the problem.

Looking for the problem's source within messages may be far easier than looking for it in the channels through which they are sent, especially the informal channels. In many cases, the human resource management system is a good place to begin the problem-solving process since this system is responsible for initial and subsequent messages pertaining to promotions, pay, managerial behavior, and the like. Consider our example of the organization that initially tells its employees that training is a high priority. After receiving this message, employees may start working for a department manager who perceives training as detracting from accomplishing short-run productivity standards. Consequently, the manager may downgrade the employees' performance evaluations when they try to take advantage of training and development opportunities. In this case, the manager's actions are inconsistent with the messages employees have received, and the employees may feel that their psychological contracts with the organization have been violated. However, finding the root causes of these types of problems can be a challenging task for managers.

IMPLICATIONS

The model presented in this article goes beyond the current literature by providing a framework by which organizations can develop employee brands and turn them into a source of competitive advantage. The brand-developing process centers on the messages the organization sends and the processing of those messages in its employees' psyches. The messages employees receive must be aligned with the employees' organizational experiences if the psychological contract is to be upheld. Therefore, the conscious development of organizational messages is the fundamental building block in this process.

The messages must then be delivered through appropriate message sources. The following guidelines provide a starting point in this process:

- Organizational messages should be carefully thought out and planned in much the same way mission and vision statements are thought out and planned.
- The organizational messages should reflect the organization's mission and values.
- Messages directed toward external constituencies must be in line with the messages sent to employees.
- Messages directed toward external constituencies should be sent internally as well.
- The design of recruitment and selection systems should incorporate messages that consistently and frequently reflect the brand and organizational image.
- The compensation system should incorporate messages that consistently and frequently reflect the brand and organizational image. For instance, managers in organizations that value training must be held accountable when they fail to train and develop their employees.

- Training and development systems should help managers and employees internalize their organization's mission and values and help them understand how the mission and values pertain to their roles in their organization. This should enable them to more effectively articulate messages that consistently and frequently reflect the brand and organizational image.
- Advertising and public relations systems should communicate messages that consistently and frequently reflect the brand and organizational image.
- Managers should be taught the importance of communicating messages that are consistent with their organization's mission, vision, policies, and practices.
- Performance management systems should address inconsistencies between practices and policies to minimize violations of employees' psychological contracts.
- Accurate and specific job previews should be given to new employees so that realistic expectations are incorporated into their psychological contracts.
- Corporate culture (artifacts, patterns of behavior, management norms, values and beliefs, and assumptions) should reinforce the messages employees receive.
- Individual output should be measured and analyzed to determine if there are message-related problems at the departmental, divisional, or organizational levels.
- Individual messages should be continually examined for consistency with other messages.
- Message channels should be examined to ensure consistency of message delivery.
- In the event that messages need to be changed or psychological contracts altered, organizations must take careful steps in rewriting the messages (Rousseau, 1995).
- Measures should be used to assess outcomes such as customer retention, service quality, turnover, and employee satisfaction and performance.

SUMMARY AND CONCLUSION

This article describes a model that contributes to the conceptualization and understanding of the employee branding process–a process by which employees internalize the desired brand image and are motivated to project the image to customers and other organizational constituents. The messages employees take in and process influence (1) the extent to which they perceive their psychological contracts with the organization to be fulfilled and (2) the degree to which they understand and are motivated to deliver the desired level of customer service. In so doing, they drive the formation of the employee brand.

Message consistency is important for effective brand formation. Employees receiving consistent messages are more likely to perceive that their psychological contracts have been upheld and to develop a sense of trust in the organization. Consistent messages also enable employees to understand the desired brand and organizational image. Favorable consequences likely to emanate from successful employee branding programs include reduced employee turnover, enhanced employee satisfaction and performance, increased service quality, higher levels of customer retention, and an increase in favorable word-of-mouth communication. Organizations can monitor the consequences of the employee branding process through the proposed feedback loop.

We hope that an enhanced understanding of the employee branding process as developed in our model will lead to the development of consistent messages within the organizational system. Effective implementation of employee branding programs will help employees internalize the desired brand image and motivate them to deliver that image to their customers and other organizational constituents.

REFERENCES

Adams, J. S. (1963). Toward an understanding of inequity. *Journal of Abnormal Psychology, 67*, 422-436.

Allen, N. J., & Meyer, J. P. (1990). Organizational socialization tactics: A longitudinal analysis to newcomer commitment and role expectations. *Academy of Management Journal, 33*, 847-858.

American Society for Quality Control. (1988, October). *Consumers' perceptions concerning the quality of American products and service.* (Publication No. Y711). Author.

Berry, L. L. (1981). The employee as customer. *Journal of Retail Banking, 3*, 25-28.

Berry, L. L., & Parasuraman, A. (1991). *Marketing services: Competing through quality.* New York: Free Press.

Bone, P. F. (1995). Word-of-mouth effects on short-term and long-term product judgments. *Journal of Business Research, 32*, 213-223.

Brown, S. W. (2003, January/February). Start with the customer: At top-performing service companies, the customer always comes first. *Marketing Management*, pp. 12-13.

Burns, J. M. (1978). *Leadership*. New York: Harper.

Estell, L. (2002). Branded for life. *Incentive, 176*(9), 42-45.

Farrell, J. (2002). Promises worth keeping. *Incentive, 175*(5), 38.

Frook, J. E. (2001). Burnish your brand from the inside. *B to B, 86*(8), 1-2.

Folger, R., & Konovsky, M. A. (1989). Effects of procedural and distributive justice on reactions to pay raise decisions. *Academy of Management Journal, 32,* 115-130.

Freiberg, K., & Freiberg, J. (1996). *Nuts! Southwest Airlines' crazy recipe for business and personal success.* Austin, TX: Bard Press.

Frost, F. A., & Kumar, M. (2000). INTSERVQUAL–An internal adaptation of the GAP model in a large service organization. *Journal of Services Marketing, 14,* 358-377.

George, W. R. (1977). The retailing of services–A challenging future. *Journal of Retailing, 53*(3), 85-98.

Gephart, M. A., Marsick, V. J., Van Buren, M. E., & Spiro, M. S. (1996). Learning organizations come alive. *Training and Development, 50,* 35-45.

Goetting, S. (2000, June/July). Aligning external and internal messages: Marketing a learning program to an internal audience. *Strategic Communication Management,* pp. 18-21.

Gratton, L. (1998, June). The new rules of HR strategy. *HR Focus,* pp. 13-14.

Greene, W. E., Walls, G. D., & Schrest, L. J. (1994). Internal marketing: The key to external marketing success. *Journal of Services Marketing, 8*(4), 5-13.

Gronroos, C. (1981). Internal marketing–An integral part of marketing theory. In J. H. Donnelly & W. E. George (Eds.), *Marketing of Services,* pp. 236-238. Chicago, IL: American Marketing Association.

Hamel, G., & Prahalad, C. K. (1994). *Competing for the future.* Cambridge, MA: Harvard Business School Press.

Herr, P. M., Kardes, F. R., & Kim, J. (1991). Effects of word-of-mouth and product-attribute information on persuasion: An accessibility-diagnosticity perspective. *Journal of Consumer Research, 17,* 454-462.

Heskett, J. L., & Jones, T. O. (1994). Putting the service-profit chain to work. *Harvard Business Review, 72,* 164-170.

Huselid, M. A., Jackson, S. E., & Schuler, R. S. (1997). Technical and strategic HRM effectiveness as determinants of firm performance. *Academy of Management Journal, 40,* 171-188.

Jones, G. R., & George, J. M. (2003). *Contemporary management.* New York: McGraw Hill.

Joseph, W. B. (1996). Internal marketing builds service quality. *Journal of Health Care Marketing, 16*(1), 54-60.

Katz, D., & Kahn, R. L. (1978). *The social psychology of organizations.* New York: John Wiley & Sons.

Kelman, H. C. (1958). Compliance, identification and internationalization: Three process of attitude change. *Journal of Conflict Resolution, 2,* 51-60.

Kerin, R. A., Berkowitz, E. N., Hartley, S. W., & Rudelius, W. (2003). *Marketing* (7th ed.). Boston, MA: McGraw Hill Irwin.

Kotler, P. (2003). *A framework for marketing management.* Upper Saddle River, NJ: Prentice Hall.

Krishnan, B., & Hartline, M. D. (2001). Brand equity: Is it more important in services? *Journal of Services Marketing, 15*(5), 328-342.

Mathis, R. L., & Jackson, J. H. (2000). *Human resource management*. Cincinnati, OH: Southwestern College Publishing.

McKenzie, A. (2001). Effective employment branding. *Strategic Communication Management, 5*(4), 22-26.

Mitchell, C. (2002, January). Selling the brand inside. *Harvard Business Review*, pp. 99-105.

Noe, R. A., Hollenbeck, J. R., Gerhart, B., & Wright, P. M. (2003*). Human resource management: Gaining a competitive advantage* (4th ed.). New York: McGraw Hill.

Ott, J. (1989). *The organizational culture perspective*. Pacific Grove, CA: Brooks Cole Publishing.

Parasuraman, A., Zeithaml, V., & Berry, L. (1985). A conceptual model of services quality and its implications for future research. *Journal of Marketing, 49*, 41-50.

Parasuraman, A., Zeithaml, V., & Berry, L. (1988). SERVQUAL: A multiple-item scale for measuring customer perceptions of service quality. *Journal of Retailing, 64*(1), 12-39.

Paul, R. J., & Niehoff, B. P. (2000). Workplace sabotage and psychological contracts: A review of research and recommendations for managers. *Journal of Business and Public Affairs, 27*(1), 20-26.

Rafiq, M., & Ahmed, P. K. (1993). The scope of internal marketing: Defining the boundary between marketing and human resource management. *Journal of Marketing Management, 9*, 219-232.

Rafiq, M., & Ahmed, P. K. (2000). Advances in the internal marketing concept: Definition, synthesis and extension. *Journal of Services Marketing, 14*, 449-462.

Reardon, K., & Enis, B. (1990). Establishing a companywide customer orientation through persuasive internal marketing. *Management Communication Quarterly, 3*, 376-388.

Robbins, S. (1994). *Management* (4th ed.). Englewood Cliffs, NJ: Prentice Hall.

Robinson, S. L. (1996). Trust and breach of the psychological contract. *Administrative Science Quarterly, 41*, 574-599.

Robinson, S., & Rousseau, D. (1994). Violating the psychological contract: Not the exception, but the norm. *Journal of Organizational Behavior, 15*, 245-259.

Rousseau, D. (1995). *Psychological contracts in organizations: Understanding written and unwritten agreements*. Thousand Oaks, CA: Sage Publications.

Southwest Airlines. (2003, January 22). *Southwest Airlines reports fourth quarter earning and 30th consecutive year of profitability*. News Release. Retrieved April 13, 2003, from http://www.iflyswa.com/about_swa/press/prindex.html

Vroom, V. (1964). *Work and motivation*. New York: John Wiley.

Winter, J. P. (1985). Getting your house in order with internal marketing: A marketing prerequisite. *Health Marketing Quarterly, 3*(1), 69-77.

Yukl, G. (1989). *Leadership in organizations* (2nd ed.). New York: Academic Press.

Exploring the Internal Customer Mind-Set of Marketing Personnel

Felicia G. Lassk

Northeastern University

Karen Norman Kennedy

University of Alabama–Birmingham

Jerry R. Goolsby

Loyola University

Felicia G. Lassk, PhD, is Assistant Professor of Marketing and Joseph G. Reisman Research Professor, College of Business Administration, Northeastern University, 360 Huntington Avenue, 202 Hayden, Boston, MA 02115 (E-mail: f.lassk@neu.edu). Her research has appeared in the *Journal of the Academy of Marketing Science, Journal of Personal Selling and Sales Management, Industrial Marketing Management*, and the *Journal of Business Research*.

Karen Norman Kennedy, PhD, is Assistant Professor of Marketing, School of Business Administration, University of Alabama at Birmingham, Birmingham, AL 35294 (E-mail: kkennedy@uab.edu). Her research has appeared in the *Journal of the Academy of Marketing Science, Journal of Personal Selling and Sales Management, Industrial Marketing Management*, and the *Journal of Services Marketing*.

Jerry R. Goolsby, PhD, is the Hilton/Baldridge Chair and Professor of Marketing and Eminent Scholar in Music Industry Studies, College of Business Administration, Loyola University of New Orleans, 6363 St. Charles Avenue, Box 15, New Orleans, LA 70118 (E-mail: jgoolsby@loyno.edu). Dr. Goolsby has previously served on the faculties of Oklahoma State University and the University of South Florida. His research has appeared in the *Journal of Marketing, Journal of Marketing Research*, and the *Journal of the Academy of Marketing Science*.

[Haworth co-indexing entry note]: "Exploring the Internal Customer Mind-Set of Marketing Personnel." Lassk, Felicia G., Karen Norman Kennedy, and Jerry R. Goolsby. Co-published simultaneously in *Journal of Relationship Marketing* (Best Business Books, an imprint of The Haworth Press, Inc.) Vol. 3, No. 2/3, 2004, pp. 89-106; and: *Internal Relationship Management: Linking Human Resources to Marketing Performance* (ed: Michael D. Hartline, and David Bejou) Best Business Books, an imprint of The Haworth Press, Inc., 2004, pp. 89-106. Single or multiple copies of this article are available for a fee from The Haworth Document Delivery Service [1-800-HAWORTH, 9:00 a.m. - 5:00 p.m. (EST). E-mail address: docdelivery@haworthpress.com].

http://www.haworthpress.com/web/JRM
Digital Object Identifier: 10.1300/J366v03n02_06

SUMMARY. With a traditional focus on external customers, marketing personnel could be expected to provide a leadership role in bringing an internal customer focus to the organization. In this study, we focus on the internal customer mind-set (ICMS) of marketing personnel and how this might impact the organization. We present a theoretically driven model that integrates current human resources literature by representing ICMS as a mediator of job satisfaction/organizational commitment and job performance/turnover intentions. The most notable results are found between ICMS and job performance, through both direct and indirect effects. Future research and study limitations are discussed. *[Article copies available for a fee from The Haworth Document Delivery Service: 1-800-HAWORTH. E-mail address: <docdelivery@haworthpress.com> Website: <http://www.HaworthPress. com> © 2004 by The Haworth Press, Inc. All rights reserved.]*

KEYWORDS. Internal marketing, internal customers, customer mind-set, marketing professionals, job performance, job satisfaction

Traditionally, marketing personnel have been the champions of the external customer within their organization, a role that has lead these professionals to focus on the external environment of the firm (Kohli and Jaworski, 1990; Kotler, 2000; Borden, 1964). As organizations realize the importance of employees as internal customers, the needs of the external, paying customer must be linked ever closer to the workers within the firm, producing a chain-of-customers cascading through the organization (Gummesson, 1991; Schonberger, 1990). Gummesson (2002) explains "[a]n employee's ability to influence and satisfy the needs of others inside the organization is considered an antecedent to external customer satisfaction. Only if internal customer relationships work can the quality of the outcome be excellent, thus creating satisfied, or even better, delighted external customers" (pp. 45-46).

For this high level of customer satisfaction to occur, the needs of external customers must be tightly coupled with an organization's internal efforts. Supporting this alignment, a culture of internal and external customer service must be present in which marketing personnel extend their external, boundary spanning responsibilities to include a greater understanding of internal customers and processes. To investigate the extent to which customer oriented beliefs have permeated an organization's culture, Kennedy, Lassk, and Goolsby (2002) examined individual workers' adoption of both internal and external customer focus or customer mind-set (CMS) by assessing employee beliefs, an important element of organizational culture. The notion that employees believe that they must understand and satisfy internal and external customers in order to perform their job effectively is the central element of CMS. Built upon the foundations of the marketing concept (customer focus, interfunctional coordination, and long-term goal attainment), CMS is conceptualized as two components: external customer mind-set (ECMS) and internal customer mind-set (ICMS) (Kennedy, Lassk, and Goolsby, 2002).

In this study, we focus on the *internal* customer mind-set of marketing personnel. While previous research has examined the importance of internal customers and studied related employee behaviors (i.e., Brown et al., 2002; Gronroos, 1981; 1990; Gummesson, 1991; Hurley and Hult, 1998; Mohr-Jackson, 1992; Slater and Narver, 1995), we investigate marketing personnel's beliefs and link those beliefs to important job outcomes at the individual level. As we have noted, marketing personnel have historically been externally focused and we would expect these professionals to rate their beliefs about understanding and satisfying external customers as quite high with little variation in the group. With this traditional focus on external customers, marketing personnel could be expected to provide a leadership role in bringing an internal customer focus to the organization. Therefore, our contribution in this manuscript is examining the role of an internal focus for marketing personnel and how that might impact the organization. For these reasons, we believe the study of marketing personnel to be especially important.

We present a theoretically driven model that integrates current human resources literature by presenting ICMS as a mediator of job satisfaction/organizational commitment and job performance/turnover intentions. Specifically, we (1) explicate a theoretically supported model that presents ICMS as a mediator of job outcome relationships, (2) discuss our empirical findings and (3) close with suggestions for future research.

A MEDIATING MODEL OF ICMS

Historically, the impact of employee beliefs on job outcomes has been modeled through a direct effects model. Recently, however, more complex mediating models have been presented, in which certain beliefs are hypothesized to intervene between job characteristics and job outcomes (Judge et al. 2001, Linden, Wayne and Sparrowe 2000; Onne 2001; Yousef 2000). In our investigation of internal customer mind-set

(ICMS), we examine its mediating effect on the relationships between two independent variables (job satisfaction and organizational commitment) and two dependent variables (job performance and turnover intentions).

A mediating model suggests that ICMS mediates the relationship between two job factors, because ICMS could be expected to enhance the effect of one variable on another. For example, while it is logical that anyone who is satisfied with his/her job should be more committed to that job, it is not intuitive that ICMS would enhance that relationship by simultaneously impacting satisfaction and turnover. Such insights, if supported, could be highly instructive to executives desiring to enhance the effect of multiple organizational factors simultaneously. Here, we investigate job satisfaction and organizational commitment as antecedents of ICMS, and job performance and turnover intentions as outcomes of ICMS (see Figure 1). First, the direct effects are hypothesized, and then the theoretical rationalizations for ICMS's mediating effect are given.

An ICMS is conceptualized as the importance an individual employee places on serving internal customers. The organizational behavior literature is grounded on the fundamental thesis that employee beliefs directly affect job outcomes such as job performance, job satisfaction and organizational commitment (cf. Vroom, 1964). Additional theoretical support for direct linkages can be drawn from research of a

FIGURE 1. The ICMS Mediating Model

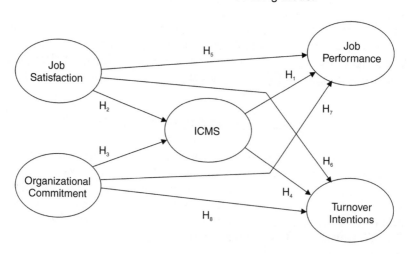

related construct, market orientation. While an empirical question, effects documented at the organizational level should, in theory, arise from the collective aggregation of effects experienced at the individual level. That is, if an organization performs better when its collective members are market oriented, it stands to reason that workers would perform better individually with a similar customer focus. Based on both literatures, we hypothesize the following direct effects.

Following the well-established theory and empirical literature, it is only reasonable to expect, as hypothesized in Kennedy, Lassk and Goolsby's (2002) initial work, that ICMS, as a belief system, should be associated with higher levels of performance (Cortada, 1993; Smith, 1990). The unified efforts resulting from cooperating with and serving other employees in the organization should increase the ability of a marketing practitioner to serve customers, thus leading to increases in traditional measures of marketing performance. In the same way that understanding external customer requirements leads to higher sales and customer satisfaction, being cognizant of internal customer requirements would be expected to lead to enhanced abilities to carry out marketing functions on behalf of external customers. For example, marketing practitioners who are cognizant of and dedicated to serving the needs of internal customers in shipping are more likely to approach a customer request from a non-adversarial position than a marketing practitioner who is relatively insensitive to the needs of the requirements of the shipping department. A heightened sense of cooperation should yield a greater ability to execute important tasks needed for success.

H_1: A marketer's level of ICMS is positively related to their job performance.

A direct relationship between ICMS and job satisfaction can also be hypothesized. Previous research has found satisfied employees are more likely to engage in behaviors that support customer service (Hartline and Ferrell, 1996; Locke and Latham, 1990; Weatherly and Tansik, 1993). Furthermore, Schneider (1980) finds evidence that job satisfaction is strongly associated with an employees' desire to deliver good service. Drawing inspiration from this research, we expect that employees who are more satisfied with their job are more likely to have beliefs that they have a responsibility to understand and meet their internal customers' expectations, while fulfilling their job task. Marketing workers with higher levels of ICMS, by being cognizant of and responsive to the demands of internal workers, should increase the opportunities to extract satisfaction from the job, suggesting a direct linkage. Instead of them experiencing the conflict that arises from insensitivity to other internal customer needs, individuals high in ICMS should experience a workplace less burdened by angst and turmoil, thus leading to higher levels of satisfaction. Research on customer oriented behaviors has found positive relationships with job satisfaction (Bateham and Organ, 1983; Hoffman and Ingram, 1992; Siguaw, Brown and Widing, 1994), suggesting a linkage to ICMS.

H_2: A marketer's job satisfaction is positively related to their level of ICMS.

We expect organizational commitment to be positively related to an internal customer mind-set. Empirical support for this hypothesis comes from the positive relationship found between organizational commitment and shared values (Hartline, Maxham III and McKee, 2000; Meglino, Ravlin, and Adkins, 1989). Shared values are one important element of the organizational culture. To the extent that a marketer works to foster positive relationships across the organization, as reflected in higher ICMS scores, organizational commitment should be enhanced directly. Specifically, personnel who derive intrinsic reward from satisfying and creating value for their internal customers will be more committed to working in an environment where they can add value and have their intrinsic needs met. Employees will be more committed and want to continue working in an environment where they can add value and have their intrinsic needs met.

H_3: A marketer's organizational commitment is positively related to their level of ICMS.

For similar reasons to organizational commitment, we contend that ICMS will be related to turnover intentions. Intention to turnover should be lowered when marketers feel connected to the organization and are committed to continuing the relationship. ICMS should enhance that commitment directly via the connection to enhanced relationships in the organization, and the attractiveness of other employment opportunities would have to be increased to offset the loss of relationships that have been created in the organization. As such, we expect to find a significant, if modest, relationship between ICMS and intention to turnover.

H_4: A marketer's level of ICMS is negatively related to their turnover intentions.

Much research has investigated the causality of the relationship between job satisfaction and job performance (Judge et al., 2001). Judge et al. (2001) identified seven different models of relationships between job satisfaction and job performance. Their meta-analysis found support for a .30 correlation between the constructs. Bagozzi (1980) and Babakus et al. (1999) provide support for the direct positive relationship between job performance and job satisfaction. In addition, Brown and Peterson's (1993) meta-analysis study found empirical support for a positive relationship between job performance and job satisfaction. While the causal direction can be modeled in a host of ways, including direct, reciprocal and curvilinear (cf. Judge et al., 2001), we investigate a positive, direct relationship from job satisfaction to job performance, consistent with much of the marketing literature.

We contend that ICMS will substantially alter the coefficient observed in the direct model, because ICMS should amplify the impact of job satisfaction on job performance by providing a channel in which job satisfaction, extracted from nurturing relationships with other employees and functional areas, can be manifest in increased job performance. Because ICMS enhances a marketer's ability to work internally to create positive relationships across the organization, it should be a central mechanism through which a marketer is effective. Therefore, we contend that the presence of ICMS rather than just job satisfaction, drives increases in performance. We expect that much of the variance between job satisfaction and job performance will be explained by ICMS, thus reducing the direct relationship.

H_5: The direct effect of job satisfaction on job performance will be partially mediated by the marketer's level of ICMS.

Both conceptually and empirically, employees' job satisfaction has been negatively linked to turnover intentions (Babakus et al., 1999; Boles, Johnston and Hair, 1997; Netemeyer, Johnston and Burton, 1990; Sager, 1994). That is, employees who are not satisfied with their job are more likely to leave the organization than those who are satisfied with their job. We contend that ICMS will explain much of the variance in this relationship, because ICMS enhances job satisfaction and lowers turnover intentions simultaneously by developing value-adding relationships across the organization that allows the marketer to extract greater meaning from his/her work, thus enhancing job satisfaction and lowering turnover intentions simultaneously.

H_6: The direct effect of job satisfaction on turnover intentions will be partially mediated by the marketer's level of ICMS.

Research has supported direct relationships between organizational commitment and job performance (Babakus et al., 1999; DeCotiis and Summers, 1987). Conceptually, individuals who are committed to their work should perform at higher levels than individuals who view their relationship with the organization as tenuous. We contend that ICMS partially mediates the relationships between job satisfaction and organizational commitment and job performance, because marketers with higher levels of ICMS should enhance the relationships in the organization that lead to commitment and which simultaneously enhance performance. To the extent that marketers are able through advanced levels of ICMS to master the network of relationships and dynamics in the organization, higher levels of commitment and enhanced performance should emerge from this expertise.

H_7: The direct effect of organizational commitment on job performance will be partially mediated by the marketer's level of ICMS.

The organizational behavior literature has long documented the intuitive insight that the more connected an individual is to an organization the less likely the individual is to quit the organization (cf. Vroom, 1964). Confirming results have been found in the sales management literature (cf. Teas, 1980, Sager, 1994) and with market orientation (Babakus et al., 1999; Johnston et al., 1990; Siguaw, Brown and Widing, 1994). We expect that ICMS will mediate this relationship because the development of networks in the organization enhances the marketer's value to the organization. This enhanced value makes leaving more difficult for two reasons. First, commitment should enhance the individual's desire to increase ICMS in the organization. Second, organizations generally reward employees with higher levels of performance, which makes changing jobs more difficult as the individual's value to his/her current organization is higher than would be that of an organization in which this ICMS has yet to be mastered.

H_8: The direct effect of organizational commitment on turnover intentions will be partially mediated by the marketer's level of ICMS.

RESEARCH METHODOLOGY

Marketing personnel were chosen for this study primarily because of their traditional role as external customer advocates and the potential leadership role they could take in an organization developing an internal customer orientation. The marketing personnel sample was drawn from members of the American Marketing Association (A.M.A.) and a university's Marketing Department mailing list that includes marketing alumni and executive roundtable members. Both lists were used to include a wide variety of organizations, both local and nationwide as well as large and small organizations. By sampling such a variety of organizations, a more generalizable portrayal of marketing personnel's beliefs and attitudes was expected. Systematic samples of 300 AMA members and 310 Marketing Department mailing list members were selected for the sample. Seventy-six questionnaires were returned from the A.M.A. sample while 98 questionnaires were returned from the Marketing Department sample. After excluding non-delivered returns and insufficiently completed questionnaires, the response rates were approximately 25% and 31% for the A.M.A. and Marketing Department samples, respectively. A combined sample of 138 marketing personnel was achieved.

The majority of respondents are managers (63.8%), have college degrees (91.1%), and have been in their current position for five or more years (60%). Most respondents (77.5%) work for service firms representing a variety of industries (financial institutions, healthcare providers, retailing operations, etc.). Following Armstrong and Overton's (1977) procedures for estimating the effects of non-response bias, t-tests and cross-tabulations of key questions were made for the first and second waves of data collection. No statistically significant differences between early and late respondents at the .05 level were found.

Measures

All measures used in this study are previously published measures (see Table 1). All scales were found to exhibit acceptable reliability,

TABLE 1. Measurement Scales

Construct	Citation	Number of Items	Anchors	Coefficient Alpha
ICMS	Kennedy, Lassk and Goolsby (2002)	4	1 = Strongly Disagree 6 = Strongly Agree	.87
Job Satisfaction	Adapted from Churchill, Ford and Walker (1974)	7	1 = Very Dissatisfied 6 = Very Satisfied	.83
Perceived Job Performance	Kennedy, Lassk and Burns (2001)	10	1 = Never 6 = Always	.90
Organizational Commitment	Mowday, Steers and Porter (1979)	6	1 = Strongly Disagree 6 = Strongly Agree	.92
Turnover Intentions	Donnelly and Ivancevich (1975)	3	1 = Strongly Disagree 6 = Strongly Agree	.94

with Cronbach's α above the recommended .70 level (Nunnally and Bernstein, 1994). Table 2 presents the correlation matrix of the constructs showing that each construct, while statistically correlated, does represent a distinct measure.

RESULTS

To investigate the hypothesized relationships, regression analysis was employed. The results are shown in Table 3. Judd and Kenny (1981) describe three relationships that have to hold to gauge the mediating relationships of ICMS: (1) the independent variables (job satisfaction and organizational commitment) should be significantly related to the mediator variable (ICMS), (2) the independent variables should be related to the dependent variables (job performance and turnover intentions), and (3) the mediating variable should be associated with the dependent variable with the independent variable included in the regression equation. Thus for the relationship with ICMS as a mediator between job satisfaction and job performance, the following equations should hold (Yousef, 2000):

$$(1) \quad I = c + \beta_1 JS + \varepsilon$$

$$(2) \quad P = c + \beta_1 JS + \varepsilon$$

$$(3) \quad P = c + \beta_1 JS + \beta_2 I + \varepsilon$$

where I = ICMS, JS = Job Satisfaction, P = Job Performance, and c = Constant.

TABLE 2. Correlation Matrix

	ICMS	Job Satisfaction	Job Performance	Organizational Commitment	Turnover Intentions
ICMS	1.00				
Job Satisfaction	.34**	1.00			
Job Performance	.64**	.42**	1.00		
Organizational Commitment	.34**	.75**	.47**	1.00	
Turnover Intentions	−.20*	−.63**	−.23**	−.68**	1.00

Note: *p < .05, **p < .001

If β_1 in equation 3 is not significant, then the mediator relationship holds. If β_1 in equation 3 is significant, then a partial mediating relationship is found. That is, for partial mediation, both the direct relationship between the dependent and independent variable holds, as well as the indirect relationship through the mediator.

Prior to examining the mediating relationships, the proposed direct relationships H_1-H_4 were investigated. The relationship between ICMS and job performance is tested in Models 1 and 2 as reported in Table 3. The relationship is found to be significant at $p < .01$ (supporting H_1). Hypothesis H_2 is supported. Job satisfaction is positively related to ICMS (see Model 1, equation 1.). Organizational commitment is positively related to ICMS (supporting H_3). Conversely, the relationship between ICMS and turnover intentions (H_4) is not supported (see Model 3 and 4, equation 3 in Table 3).

Model 1 and Model 2 results show partial mediating relationships, supporting H_5 and H_7. All three equations for each model are significant. Since both job satisfaction and ICMS are significant in Model 1, equation 3, both the direct and indirect relationships are supported. Thus, ICMS partially mediates the relationship between job satisfaction and job performance, since the direct relationship between job satisfaction and job performance is also significant. Similar results are found for Model 2 where ICMS is shown to partially mediate the relationship between organizational commitment and job performance.

Since equation 3 in Models 3 and 4 results in non-significant coefficients for the ICMS-turnover intentions relationship, H_6 and H_8 are not supported. Thus, mediation is not supported for the models with turnover intentions as an outcome. Based on these analyses, improving marketing personnel's performance requires higher levels of organizational

TABLE 3. Results of Regression Analyses

Job Performance Models:

Dependent Variable	Independent Variables	R^2	β
Model 1			
(1) ICMS	Constant	.11	16.37*
	Job Satisfaction		.18*
(2) Performance	Constant	.18	44.01*
	Job Satisfaction		.39*
(3) Performance	Constant	.46	28.51*
	Job Satisfaction		.21*
	ICMS		.95*
Model 2			
(1) ICMS	Constant	.12	17.42*
	Commit		.17*
(2) Performance	Constant	.22	45.45*
	Commit		.40*
(3) Performance	Constant	.48	29.48*
	Commit		.24*
	ICMS		.92*

Turnover Intentions Models:

Dependent Variable	Independent Variables	R^2	β
Model 3			
(1) ICMS	Constant	.12	16.37*
	Job Satisfaction		.18*
(2) Turnover	Constant	.39	32.93*
	Job Satisfaction		-.66*
(3) Turnover	Constant	.40	24.30*
	Job Satisfaction		-.60*
	ICMS		.03
Model 4			
(1) ICMS	Constant	.12	17.42*
	Commit		.17*
(2) Turnover	Constant	.47	22.32*
	Commit		-.61*
(3) Turnover	Constant	.47	21.04*
	Commit		-.62*
	ICMS		.11

*$p < .05$

commitment and job satisfaction in order to increase the level of ICMS and in turn increase the levels of job performance. Table 4 summarizes the hypotheses results.

DISCUSSION

While the marketer's job has been primarily to focus on the satisfaction of external customers, interest in the internal focus of marketing personnel has only recently garnered empirical attention in the literature. While marketing theorists have long noted that an internal customer focus could be important to job performance, this study represents the first attempt to model those effects. Based on the customer mind-set scale of Kennedy, Lassk, and Goolsby (2002), the potential mediating effect of an internal customer mind-set (ICMS) was investigated.

The results suggest that, as theorized, ICMS does have notable effects on important job outcomes, which may add to the understanding of the work environment of marketing personnel. Clearly the most notable effects are those found between ICMS and job performance, through both direct and indirect effects. The direct effect suggests that marketers with higher levels of an internal focus perform better than do those with lower levels. It reasons that marketers who master the art of serving individuals inside the organization can create an environment in which others want to reciprocate, allowing the marketer to better serve his/her customers and increase his/her performance. While the marketing discipline has been rightfully concerned with an external focus for decades, this finding infers that marketing executives would be wise to instill a

TABLE 4. Hypothesis Testing Results

Hypothesis	Description	Result
H_1	ICMS → Performance	Supported
H_2	Job Satisfaction → ICMS	Supported
H_3	Commitment → ICMS	Supported
H_4	ICMS → Turnover Intentions	Not Supported
H_5	ICMS mediates Job Sat → Performance	Supported
H_6	ICMS mediates Job Sat → Turnover Intentions	Not Supported
H_7	ICMS mediates Commitment → Performance	Supported
H_8	ICMS mediates Commitment → Turnover Intentions	Not Supported

culture of internal service focus among marketing personnel. That is, rather than demand that internal employees serve them, marketing personnel should understand the needs and wants of internal customers, so that an appreciation of their situation and limitations can help them serve the organization and all of its customers more thoroughly. This finding of a common ground, on which both the organization and its customers are served, may be a critical factor in improving performance. Far too often marketing personnel are charged with being insensitive to internal customers' needs, causing chaos in areas such as service, distribution and manufacturing, all in the name of serving the external customer. If organizations have focused solely on satisfying external customers to the detriment of organizational processes, promoting an ICMS would seem valuable.

ICMS's indirect effects on job performance also offer some interesting insights. Support was found for a mediating ICMS relationship between job satisfaction and job performance, as well as one between commitment and job performance. These two findings infer that a synergistic relationship exists among ICMS, commitment, and job satisfaction, so that when combined, they yield higher job performance. Though tentative, the results suggest that job satisfaction and commitment give rise to higher levels of ICMS. Marketers who are satisfied with their jobs and committed to working for the organization are likely to find greater value in developing the internal networks needed to prosper. This, in turn, leads to decreased turmoil and increased camaraderie, thereby causing employees to embrace a stance toward serving the needs of internal customers. This process results in improved job performance–an outcome that is certainly noteworthy to marketing executives.

Much discussion has been made in the marketing literature about the importance of organizational culture in creating a market and/or customer orientation. The positive results emerging from this preliminary study suggest that ICMS may be a critical factor in developing that culture. As such, researchers pursuing the study of culture might be instructed to include the examination of an internal customer orientation in their research.

The research failed to show a direct linkage or mediating effect between ICMS and turnover intentions. Given the strong direct relationship between commitment and job satisfaction with turnover intentions, the relationship between ICMS and turnover intentions may be overshadowed by commitment and job satisfaction. The theoretical linkages hypothesized in this research are tentative and exploratory, and future research may scrutinize these relationships to determine more precisely the operative mechanisms. The relationship may also be confounded by the increase in job performance associated with ICMS, which could also affect turnover intentions. Clearly, more work is needed to dissect these complex relationships.

LIMITATIONS AND DIRECTIONS FOR FUTURE RESEARCH

As with all research, limitations exist with our study. While this study provides an initial examination of ICMS and its outcomes, additional research is needed to establish the proposed linkages. We acknowledge that the relationships revealed by this study may be susceptible to common method variance. All of the measurement scales are self-report. Also, by using a sample from a variety of industries, possible increases in organizational and environmental factors may be present in the study results.

These limitations can be addressed in future research. First, a comprehensive causal model that can simultaneously investigate the numerous pathways uncovered in this research is needed. While our research examined the mediating effect of ICMS, other more robust models can be explored, including an expanded list of antecedents and outcomes. For example, because ICMS is measured at the individual level, other personality and demographic characteristics could be investigated as antecedents and external customer satisfaction could be studied as an outcome. Second, we recommend that future research include organizational measures of marketing personnel's performance, using multiple methods and measures. And, while our research is most applicable to marketing employees, future research could expand this view to include organization-wide employees. The ICMS construct enables management to measure the extent of beliefs related to serving customers throughout the organization. Understanding where internal customer relationships are strong or weak will help the organization focus training efforts on those employees that need improvement. In addition, by expanding research to all employees, the consistency of ICMS scores throughout an organization can gauge the strength of its customer-oriented culture (Kennedy, Lassk and Goolsby, 2002).

Finally, previous research has shown that training, concerning both internal and external customers, can improve employees' customer orientation. Thus, we suggest that future research empirically investigate which type of customer orientation training is most effective in instilling a customer focus throughout the organization. This and previous research on market orientation show that organizations with a customer focus yield greater success for both employees and the organization.

In summary, ICMS, while a nascent construct in the discipline, seems to show promise as a potentially important variable in the study of job performance and organizational culture in marketing. While marketers have concentrated on executives and their instillation of customer and market orientations in organizations, this research shows that studying the beliefs of marketing's operating personnel may hold promise in efforts to understand why some marketing functions are more successful than others. In the final analysis, it is when marketing personnel are able to deliver value to customers that success is achieved, and while no one would discount the importance of executives in creating a conducive culture, studying the mind-set of marketers may open avenues in understanding how successful those executive efforts have been. Indeed, ICMS could become a managerially useful diagnostic tool for ascertaining the extent to which marketing personnel have truly embraced a culture of serving not only those customers outside, but also those inside the firm.

REFERENCES

Armstrong, J. S. and Overton, T. (1977). Estimating nonresponse bias in mail surveys. *Journal of Marketing Research, 14* (August), 396-402.

Babakus, E., Cravens, D. W., Johnston, M. W., and Moncrief, W. C. (1999). The role of emotional exhaustion in sales force attitude and behavioral relationships. *Journal of the Academy of Marketing Science*, Winter, 58-70.

Bagozzi, R. P. (1980). Performance and satisfaction in the industrial salesforce: an examination of their antecedents and simultaneity. *Journal of Marketing, 44* (June), 417-424.

Bateham, T. S. and Organ, D. W. (1983). Job satisfaction and the good soldier: the relationship between affect and employee "citizenship." *Academy of Management Journal, 36,* 587-595.

Boles, J. S., Johnston, M. W. and Hair, J. E. (1997). Role stress, work-family conflict and emotional exhaustion: interrelationships and effects on some work related consequences. *Journal of Personal Selling and Sales Management*, Winter, 17-28.

Borden, N. (1964). The concept of the marketing mix. *Journal of Advertising Research, 4* (June), 2-7.

Brown, S. P. and Peterson, R. A. (1993). Antecedents and consequences of salesperson job satisfaction: meta-analysis and assessment of causal effects. *Journal of Marketing Research, 30* (February), 63-77.

Brown, T. J., Mowen, J. C., Donavan, D. T. and Licata, J. W. (2002). The customer orientation of service workers: personality trait effects of self and supervisor performance ratings. *Journal of Marketing Research, 39* (1), 110-119.

Churchill, G. A., Ford, N. M., and Walker, O. C. (1974). Measuring the job satisfaction of industrial salesmen. *Journal of Marketing Research, 11* (August), 254-260.

Cortada, J. W. (1993). *TQM for sales and marketing management.* New York: McGraw-Hill.

DeCotiis, T. A. and Summers, T. P. (1987). A path analysis of a model of the antecedents and consequences of organizational commitment. *Human Relations, 40* (7), 445-470.

Donnelly, J. H. and Ivancevich, J. M. (1975). Role clarity and the salesman. *Journal of Marketing, 39* (January), 71-74.

Gronroos, C. (1981). Internal marketing–an integral part of marketing theory. In Marketing of Services. Eds. J. H. Donnelly and W. R. George. Chicago, IL: American Marketing Association. 236-238.

Gronroos, C. (1990). *Service management and marketing.* Lexington, MA: Lexington Books.

Gummesson, E. (1991). Marketing-orientation revisited: the crucial role of the part-time marketer. *European Journal of Marketing, 25* (2), 60-75.

Gummesson, E. (2002). Relationship marketing in the new economy. *Journal of Relationship Marketing, 1* (1), 37-57.

Hartline, M. D., Maxham III, J. G. and McKee, D. O. (2000). Corridors of influence in the dissemination of customer-oriented strategy to customer contact service employees. *Journal of Marketing, 64* (April), 35-50.

Hartline, M. D. and Ferrell, O. C. (1996). The management of customer-contact service employees: an empirical investigation. *Journal of Marketing, 60* (October), 52-70.

Hoffman, K. D. and Ingram, T. N. (1992). Service provider job satisfaction and customer-oriented performance. *Journal of Services Marketing, 6* (2), 68-78.

Hurley, R. F. and Hult, G. T. M. (1998). Innovation, market orientation, and organizational learning: an integration and empirical examination. *Journal of Marketing, 62* (July), 42-54.

Johnston, M., Weckert, J., Futrell, C. M., and Black, W. C. (1990). A longitudinal assessment of the impact of selected organizational influences on salespeople's organizational commitment during early development. *Journal of Marketing Research, 27* (August), 333-344.

Judd, C. M. and Kenny, D. A. (1981). Process analysis: estimating mediation in evaluation research. *Evaluation Research, 5*, 602-619.

Judge, T. A., Thoresen, C. J., Bono, J. E., and Patton, G. K. (2001). The job satisfaction-job performance relationship: a qualitative and quantitative review. *Psychological Bulletin, 127* (3), 376-407.

Kennedy, K. N., Lassk, F. G. and Goolsby, J. R. (2002). Customer mind-set of employees throughout the organization. *Journal of the Academy of Marketing Science, 30* (2), 159-171.

Kennedy, K. N., Lassk, F. G. and Burns, M. B. (2001). A scale assessing team-based job performance in a customer-oriented environment. *Journal of Quality Management, 6*, 257-273.

Kohli, A. K. and Jaworski, B. J. (1990). Market orientation: the construct, research propositions, and managerial implications. *Journal of Marketing, 54* (April), 1-18.

Kotler, P. (2000). *Marketing Management.* Upper Saddle River, NJ: Prentice Hall.

Linden, R. C., Wayne, S. J. and Sparrowe, R. T. (2000). An examination of the mediating role of psychological empowerment on the relations between the job, interpersonal relationships, and work outcomes. *Journal of Applied Psychology, 85* (3), 407-416.

Locke, E. A. and Latham, G. P. (1990). Work motivation and satisfaction: light at the end of the tunnel. *Psychological Science, 1* (July), 240-246.

Meglino, B. M., Ravlin, E. C., and Adkins, C. L. (1989). A work values approach to corporate culture: a field test of the value congruence process and its relationship to individual outcomes. *Journal of Applied Psychology, 74* (June), 424-432.

Mohr-Jackson, I. (1992). Broadening the market orientation: an added focus on internal customers. *Human Resource Management, 30* (4), 455-467.

Mowday, R. T., Steers, R. M. and Porter, L. W. (1979). The measure of organizational commitment. *Journal of Vocational Behavior, 14* (April), 224-247.

Netemeycr, R. G., Johnston, M. W. and Burton, S. (1990). Analysis of role conflict and ambiguity in structured equations framework. *Journal of Applied Psychology, 75* (April), 148-157.

Nunnally, J. C. and Bernstein, I. H. (1994). *Psychometric theory*. New York: McGraw Hill.

Onne, J. (2001). Fairness perceptions as a moderator in the curvilinear relationships between job demands, and job performance and job satisfaction. *Academy of Management Journal, 44* (October), 1039-1050.

Porter, L. W., Steers, R. M., Mowday, R. T., and Boulian, P. V. (1974). Organizational commitment, job satisfaction, and turnover among psychiatric technicians. *Journal of Applied Psychology, 59*, 603-609.

Sager, J. K. (1994). A structural model depicting salespeople's job stress. *Journal of the Academy of Marketing Science, 22* (January), 74-84.

Schneider, B. (1980). The service organization: climate is critical. *Organizational Dynamics, 9* (Autumn), 52-65.

Schonberger, R. (1990). *Building a chain of customers: linking business functions to create the world class company*. New York: Doubleday.

Sigauw, J. A., Brown, G. and Widing III, R. E. (1994). The influence of market orientation of the firm on sales. *Journal of Marketing Research, 31* (1), 106-116.

Slater, S. F. and Narver, J. C. (1995). Market orientation and the learning organization. *Journal of Marketing, 59* (July), 63-74.

Smith, F. W. (1990). Our human side of quality. *Quality Progress, 23* (10 October), 19-22.

Teas, R. Kenneth (1980). An empirical test of linkages proposed in Walker, Churchill, and Ford model of salesforce motivation and performance. *Journal of the Academy of Marketing Science, 8* (Winter), 58-72.

Vroom, Victor H. (1964). *Work and Motivation*. New York: John Wiley & Sons.

Weatherly, K. A. and Tansink, D. A. (1993). Managing multiple demands: a role-theory examination of the behaviors of customer contact service workers. *Advances in Services Marketing and Management*, Volume 2.

Yousef, D. (2000). Organizational commitment: a mediator of the relationships of leadership behavior with job satisfaction and performance in a non-western country. *Journal of Managerial Psychology, 15* (1), 6-24.

Index

For Product Safety Concerns and Information please contact our
EU representative GPSR@taylorandfrancis.com Taylor & Francis
Verlag GmbH, Kaufingerstraße 24, 80331 München, Germany